Sister Grateful

BOUND IN AN UNEQUALLY YOKED MARRIAGE

Grace to Stay – Faith to Finish

Copyright © 2024 by Sister Grateful

Bound In An Unequally Yoked Marriage: Grace to Stay – Faith to Finish

Printed in the United States of America

ISBN: 979-8-218-11073-4

All rights reserved. No part of this book may be reproduced or transmitted in any form or by any means, electronic or mechanical, including photocopying, recording, or by any information storage and retrieval system, without permission in writing from the copyright owner.

Scripture marked ESV are from the ESV® Bible (The Holy Bible, English Standard Version®). ESV® Text Edition: 2016. Copyright © 2001 by Crossway, a publishing ministry of Good News Publishers. The ESV® text has been reproduced in cooperation with and by permission of Good News Publishers. Unauthorized reproduction of this publication is prohibited. All rights reserved.

Scripture marked NCV is taken from the New Century Version®. Copyright © 2005 by Thomas Nelson. Used by permission. All rights reserved.

Scripture marked KJV are from the King James Version, public domain.

Scripture quotations marked MSG are taken from *THE MESSAGE*, copyright © 1993, 2002, 2018 by Eugene H. Peterson. They are used with permission from NavPress. All rights reserved, represented by Tyndale House Publishers, Inc.

Scripture marked NASB95 is from New American Standard Bible®, Copyright © 1960, 1971, 1977, 1995 by The Lockman Foundation. All rights reserved.

Scripture marked NKJV is taken from the New King James Version®. Copyright © 1982 by Thomas Nelson. Used by permission. All rights reserved.

Scripture marked NIV is from THE HOLY BIBLE, NEW INTERNATIONAL VERSION®, NIV® Copyright © 1973, 1978, 1984, 2011 by Biblica, Inc. Used by permission. All rights reserved worldwide.

Disclaimer

This book is a memoir designed to provide information about the subject covered.

The book's purchaser understands that the publisher and the author are not trained to render professional services. If you require expert assistance, you should seek the services of a competent professional.

Marriages are complicated and are not as simplistic as may be viewed on the surface.

I have made every effort to make this book as complete and accurate as possible. Readers should view this text merely as a guide or reference point to ponder new ideas and not as the ultimate source of the subject or psychological or sociological information.

This book is a journey designed to educate, enlighten, and entertain. The author and publisher, however, bear no liability or responsibility for any loss or damage caused or alleged to be caused directly or indirectly by the information presented.

TO CW, my husband,

You have been God's conduit, the instrument through which He has administered my trials and lessons. Despite the numerous occasions I failed my tests, your steadfast presence has been a constant in my life.

Through you, God has granted me the opportunity to retake each failed test, enabling me to develop the characteristics and virtues of Jesus.

Your unintended part in this journey has catalyzed my spiritual growth and faith. I sincerely feel gratitude, love, and thankfulness towards you.

TABLE OF CONTENTS

INTRODUCTION — 1

CHAPTER 1 — 6
The Change

CHAPTER 2 — 16
Grave Mistake

CHAPTER 3 — 20
Understanding God's Mariage Plan

CHAPTER 4 — 29
Contemplating Divorce in a Strained Marriage

CHAPTER 5 — 37
Discerning God's Voice

CHAPTER 6 — 45
The Price of Transformation

CHAPTER 7 — 58
Transforming Barriers

CHAPTER 8 — 68
Spiritual Warfare

CHAPTER 9 — 77
Distractions

CHAPTER 10 — 85
The Evolution of Love and Faith

CHAPTER 11 — 94
My Identity in Christ

CHAPTER 12 — 101
The Sacred Wilderness — 101

CHAPTER 13 — 112
Tribulation for a Purpose

CHAPTER 14 — 122
Tracing the Roots of Marital Challenges — 122

CHAPTER 15 — 129
The Love Challenge

CHAPTER 16 — 145
Staying the Course When It's Hard

CHAPTER 17 — 167
Hearing the Heart

CHAPTER 18 — 183
Sanctuary of the Soul

CHAPTER 19 — 189
The Pursuit of Lost Connection

CHAPTER 20: — 202
The Gradual Disintegration — *202*

CHAPTER 21 — 216
Reshaping Bonds

CHAPTER 22 — 225
Divine Pathway to Healing

CHAPTER 23 — 230
Conquering the Consequences

ENDNOTES — 260

INTRODUCTION

The choices we make shape the course of our lives. Thirty-three years ago, I made two critical decisions that changed my destiny: I accepted Jesus Christ as my Savior and married an unbeliever.

Because of my first choice, giving my life to Christ, I am bound to honor my second choice, my unequally yoked marriage. The dynamics of an unequally yoked marriage have consistently presented challenges.

My marriage journey has been good but arduous, and I have given much to maintain peace. I've cried a sea of tears and been engulfed in an ocean of pain due to one ignorant decision to marry an unbeliever. Yet, these trials have not been in vain. They have served as powerful catalysts for my spiritual growth.

I've learned to walk in faith, pray with all my heart, love God unconditionally, immerse myself in His teachings, sacrifice for Jesus, and embrace self-love through the lens of God's compassion.

These hard-earned and invaluable lessons have changed me and transformed me from within.

In the following chapters, I recount my journey through the relentless pursuit of CW, my husband's affection, the folly of my reactions when it eluded me, and the cost of stepping into

God's authority to overcome the challenges inherent in such a marriage. This narrative traces how God molded me into the likeness of Christ amidst these trials.

It is of utmost importance, a matter of spiritual survival, to marry someone who shares your faith in the Lord because that person will influence you every day of your life. I contacted CW to inform him that I had finished my manuscript and sent it for review.

I hoped for his approval and welcomed any disagreements to discuss and adjust accordingly, emphasizing the importance of his consent since the story deeply involved both of us, albeit from my perspective. CW refrained from providing feedback.

God's 'Noes' are not to deny us but to protect us from our 'Yeses.'

How It All Began

In the summer of 1989, I rushed to the laundromat early on a Saturday, hoping to beat the crowd. As I pulled up, relief washed over me; the place was nearly empty, save for a young man folding clothes with his children.

After briefly greeting him, I loaded my clothes into a washer. Realizing I had forgotten laundry detergent, I approached the vending machine, inserted my money, and pulled the handle—nothing. Frustrated, I tried again to no avail.

The young man noticed my plight and called out to another man I hadn't seen before, lounging on a table across the room. The man got up, walked over, and the machine released the detergent with a simple tug. I thanked him for his help, but he just nodded and lay back on the table, closing his eyes until the young man finished his laundry.

Watching them leave, I couldn't help but notice the man who helped me. He was tall, dark-skinned, and bow-legged — just my type, yet his appearance seemed marked by life's hardships. Something was captivating about him that I couldn't shake off.

A couple of days later, while canvassing the neighborhood, I spotted him again, hastily walking alongside another man. He didn't see me as I passed by. We intersected again a few days later while I drove through the neighborhood.

I saw him, but he didn't see me; he seemed distracted, maybe even troubled, as he walked. I pondered if drugs were a part of his life, a distressing thought given his apparent kindness.

Our paths crossed once more later that week. Before heading to Gracie's, a local nightclub, I had stopped on Main Street. There he was, standing by the store. Approaching him, I inquired if he remembered our laundromat encounter; he seemed to recall it vaguely. We started a conversation so fascinating that I forgot about my evening plans.

Time flew as we talked. Getting to know CW was intriguing; his commanding presence and undeniable attractiveness captivated me. Eventually, I noted the late hour and mentioned I was about to drive home.

When he asked to accompany me home, I was elated. I laid down one condition — no intimacy, just companionship. He accepted, yet the night unfolded in unexpected ways. CW's mysterious allure seemed to fill the emptiness I had felt from my loneliness.

The morning after he departed, I found myself in a blissful daze, utterly enchanted by the love we had shared and the precious moments we had spent together. Yet, he vanished as quickly as he had appeared. Despite my efforts to locate him, he remained elusive. I resigned myself to thinking it was a one-night stand. However, fate had other plans.

About a week later, he approached me smiling while I put gas in my car. My heart leaped. He explained that he had tried to visit me several times, but I was never home. This revelation was a balm to my earlier disappointment. CW wasn't just a fleeting encounter; he had been looking for me as I had for him.

We moved in together just two weeks after meeting at the gas station. I fell deeply for CW, and it seemed he felt the same. CW, though claiming to have a driving job, rarely worked. Concerned, I suggested he find more consistent employment, which he did.

The revelation of his drug use came as a shock. One evening, he brought home crack cocaine and a pipe. I had been unaware of his addiction, having triumphed over my battle with the drug years earlier. I opened up about how Jesus healed and took the desire from me. Encouraged by my experience, I urged him to pray to Jesus for healing.

We prayed together, a heartfelt plea for liberation from his chains of addiction. Following our prayer, CW flushed the drugs down the toilet, a symbolic gesture of a new beginning. For a time, we thrived, finding joy in simpler pleasures.

But addiction is a relentless foe, and he relapsed the following month. Confronting him, I stood firm: the drugs had to go, or I would. He appeared weary of his drug use and tired of his old ways.

While I want to believe he chose me over that destructive lifestyle, part of me wonders if he was just exhausted by it all. Nonetheless, from that moment, he never touched crack cocaine again.

We found contentment in our shared life, indulging our vices in less destructive ways until The CHANGE.

CHAPTER 1

The Change

Several days before experiencing The Change, my moment of divine intervention, I was deeply immersed in thoughts about life and God. During this reflective period, I engaged in open and honest dialogues with God about various aspects of my life.

"Despite asking You into my heart a lot, my life has remained the same. I believe Jesus died for my sins, and You raised Him from the dead. I want to serve You, but the things of the world got a hold on me. I enjoy sinning. I like getting high. Drinking makes me feel good. I enjoy watching pornography, partying, and having sex with my live-in boyfriend. I don't fear You, and I don't fear death. But if You are real, please manifest Yourself to me." I rose from my knees, got my Bible, sat in bed, and began reading.

When CW walked into the room a few minutes later, I told him, "I just gave my life to Jesus. Would you like to give your life to Him, too?" He left the room and replied, "No, I'm not ready to do that."

Suddenly, a rush of random thoughts flooded my mind. If I gave my life to Jesus, I couldn't party, get high, have sex with CW, or drink anymore. His words made me think about what

I had to give up if I was serious about giving my life to Jesus. *I'm not ready either*, I said to myself. I got up, put my Bible back in the closet, and continued to live in the congregation of the dead as I had been.

On Sunday morning, three days after I had asked God to make Himself known, He showed in a dream that I was nailing Satan into a wall with a hammer. After nailing him in, I put my hands on my hips, jumped back, and said, "Nan!" Just then, Satan jumped out of the wall and entered me! Terrified, I cried out, "Jesus, Jesus, Jesus!"

As soon as I said Jesus' name that third time, the unclean spirit came out of my mouth. It was like nothing I had ever felt before. Please take a deep breath and blow it into your hand. Can you feel the force of air? That's how it felt when the evil spirit came out of me. I knew God was real after calling Jesus' name and feeling the evil spirit leave my body in that force of breath.

Upon waking, I changed quickly and rushed to church just around the corner from our apartment. After hurriedly entering the church and sitting down, the preacher asked the congregation to turn to 2 Corinthians chapter 5. As I flipped through the Bible, the page landed on 2 Corinthians Chapter 6, verse 2. My heart fervently raced and pounded as I read the passage.

I realized I was having another surreal encounter with the God of this universe. "For He says, 'AT THE ACCEPTABLE TIME I LISTENED TO YOU, AND ON THE DAY OF SALVATION, I HELPED YOU,' Behold, now is 'THE ACCEPTABLE

TIME,' BEHOLD, now is 'THE DAY OF SALVATION" (NASB95).

Intuitively, I knew this verse was a direct message from God. He told me He had heard my prayer, and this was my appointed day, January 7, 1990, to receive His help to be saved! Tears of gratitude softly cascaded down my face while I tried to grasp what was happening. When the preacher did the altar call to accept Christ Jesus as your Lord and Savior, I leaped up in excitement. I confessed and accepted Christ Jesus as my Savior; I was born again then.

For years, I lived in the congregation of the dead. I did what I wanted, said what I wanted, and slept with whoever I wanted. I spent years looking everywhere for a purpose in life.

I tried to find it in my alcoholic mother, but it was not there. Suicide failed because God's grace did not let me die. Sex was fleeting, drugs were elusive, and prostitution was shameful. I tried to find purpose in love, but that was hurtful.

I discovered that destructive anger didn't help me, and the prison was degrading. Sadly, I found religion to be evasive. And any partying I did was in vain. However, God revealed my purpose in Him on that glorious Sunday morning.

Since I've mentioned the concepts of "being saved," "born again," and "salvation," let's review their meanings.

Born Again - John 3:3

In John 3:3, Jesus tells Nicodemus, "Very truly, I tell you, no one can see the kingdom of God unless they are born again."

Being "born again" happens when God's Spirit from above connects with our spirit through faith in Jesus. This renewal of the person's inward transformation marks a radical departure from one's old life of sin to a new life in Christ.

Salvation - 2 Corinthians 6:2

"Salvation" is addressed in 2 Corinthians 6:2, which quotes, "In the time of my favor I heard you, and in the day of salvation I helped you. I tell you, now is the time of God's favor; now is the day of salvation.

Salvation refers to deliverance from sin and its consequences through Jesus Christ. It leads to reconciliation with God and eternal life.

The phrase "now is the day of salvation" underscores the immediacy and urgency of responding to God's offer of salvation. It suggests that the opportunity for redemption and reconciliation with God is available now.

Saved - Ephesians 2:8

Ephesians 2:8 states, "For it is by grace you have been saved, through faith—and this not from yourselves, it is the gift of God." "Saved" refers to an individual's spiritual salvation, which involves being rescued from the penalty of sin and granted eternal life with God.

This salvation is described as a gift from God, accessible not through human efforts or deeds but through faith in Jesus Christ. The emphasis is on God's unmerited favor (grace) as the basis for salvation, with faith being how an individual receives this divine gift.

The Weight of Sin

The Holy Spirit of God is the ultimate sin detector. The Holy Spirit was convicting me of my sin. CW and I had committed fornication (had sex) for the first time after giving my life to Christ.

After engaging in sexual activity, I experienced something I had never felt before: a guilt sensation. Instinctively, I recognized that I had sinned against God, and I wept like a child, pleading for His forgiveness.

However, my desire for CW on a physical level remained, and we continued our intimate encounters. During the third occasion, following my conversion, a verse from Matthew 10:37-38 (NASB95) echoed in my mind: "He who loves father or mother more than Me is not worthy of Me. And he who loves son or daughter more than Me is not worthy of Me. And he who doesn't take his cross and follow after Me is not worthy of Me."

I knew Jesus Christ was conveying to me that if I placed my live-in boyfriend, CW, above Him in my heart, I was unworthy because I failed to appreciate the spiritual values of salvation and expectations.

Christ demanded that He be my number one priority and that I uphold His standard of holiness, as not living a holy life meant taking God's grace in vain, as mentioned in 2 Corinthians 6:1.

Living together and engaging in sexual relations without being married weighed heavily on my conscience. I realized that I could not continue to live in sin with CW. I confronted him, insisting that we must marry to prevent further wrongdoing.

CW mentioned being married once when we first met, so I asked if he was still legally married. He responded that he did not know the status of his marriage.

Therefore, I turned to God, saying, "If he's divorced, I'll consider it a sign from You that I should marry him. If he is still married, I'll interpret it as a sign that it is not Your will for us to get married." Based on these premises, I went to the courthouse to investigate CW's marital status, but unfortunately, I found no conclusive information.

What now, Lord? What should I do? I felt the Lord tell me to fast and pray.

The next day, rather than reporting to work, I stayed home and fasted, read the Bible, and prayed, asking God for a sign regarding marriage to CW.

As I finished praying, the phone rang, and a woman asked for him.

"Who are you?" I inquired.

"Anna," she replied.

"Who?"

"Anna, CW's ex-wife."

"So, y'all are divorced?

"Yes," she replied.

"Is he aware that Y'all are divorced? He says he is unaware."

Her assurance that he knew was sufficient for me to get dressed and head to the courthouse again. I was blown away by finding the divorce decree in the microfiche machine.

God had given me the sign that it was okay to marry. I couldn't wait to tell him when he got home from work.

A Gloomy Day

I presented CW with his divorce decree as he casually strolled through the front door. Then I said, "We can get married!" I added that I could put the sexual sin of fornication behind me. His facial expression said it all: he did not want to marry me! What a crushing blow!

After thinking about Jesus' words again, "She who loves her boyfriend more than I cannot be my disciple," I knelt. I knew what to do after pouring my heart out to the Lord.

I gave CW an ultimatum: either marry me or leave. After hearing this, he reacted with anger and left. He returned later, remaining silent. His frustration stemmed from his reluctance to marry, although he had never directly said he wouldn't. After not receiving his reply for a week, I was confused about what to do next. I resolved to honor God's request to live holy. Therefore, I asked our landlord, Mr. C, if he would rent the vacant apartment to CW. Mr. C agreed he would.

My ultimatum to CW was serious. When I told him about my conversation with Mr. C, he became angry and didn't speak to me for several days. After several days, I heard him talking, saying we were breaking up because he would not marry me.

After he got off the phone, I corrected him. I told him we were not breaking up because he wouldn't marry me but because I wanted my Savior, Jesus Christ, more than I wanted to be with him. According to Jesus, I should live holy and not in sin as we were (See 1 Peter 1:16).

Wedding Nuptials

CW never directly proposed marriage. Yet, on February 26, 1990, he approached me, instructing me to prepare for a courthouse visit. It had been fifty days since my spiritual transformation. Interpreting this as a divine sign, I believed God approved my union with CW.

My happiness stemmed from prioritizing the wishes of Christ Jesus over my affection for CW. Marrying him felt like a correct step, as it meant leaving behind a life of fornication.

The Dilemma of Right Intentions, Wrong Methods: A Personal Reflection

Watching a news segment after marrying CW deeply resonated with me. The story was about a man who had been released from prison and had to meet regularly with his probation officer.

One day, he found himself unable to get to his required meeting. In a desperate move, he stole a car to drive there. He successfully met with his probation officer but was arrested when he returned to the stolen car. In watching that news segment, I could identify with him.

Although he had done the right thing by keeping his appointment, he did it the wrong way by stealing a car to get there.

As a Christian, I had done the right thing by turning my back on sin, but I did it the wrong way by marrying an unbeliever. It highlights a critical insight: even with the best intentions, if our actions contradict divine guidance, we will veer off course, leading to unintended consequences.

From giving CW an ultimatum, I've learned that pressuring someone into a significant decision like marriage can cause more harm than good. Such actions can lead to resentment, weaken the relationship, and often don't address the real issues. Understanding and respecting each other's feelings and boundaries is vital to a strong relationship.

However, when one responds with anger, withdraws emotionally, or resorts to silence, it is crucial to see these behaviors as precise indicators of one's emotional state. Neglecting these signs will lead to a breakdown of the relationship, as such reactions often signal underlying issues or unexpressed emotions that, if not addressed, will erode the connection between partners.

Don't marry if y'all cannot communicate openly and empathetically and understand each other's perspectives. Godly counseling will be a helpful step forward.

A godly, solid relationship should be based on each person being born again and mutual respect, not ultimatums.

Your present decision is shaping your future.

CHAPTER 2

Grave Mistake

After marrying CW, I was jolted by a profound realization: our union was a mistake. This epiphany was a harsh wake-up call, a slap in the face. The man I deeply loved appeared transformed.

His patience thinned, mainly when I spoke of my faith in Jesus Christ. His words, 'It doesn't take all that; you think you are better than others,' echoed in my mind, starkly contrasting my sincere desire to share God's word.

But upon reflection, I understood that it was I who had changed. My rebirth into faith infused me with a divine enthusiasm and an eagerness to share Jesus's teachings and live a life honoring God's holiness. Unfortunately, CW did not share this spiritual zeal, creating a rift in our relationship.

This strain deepened two months into our marriage when I joyfully discovered I was pregnant, only to be met with CW's lackluster response. His lack of enthusiasm, evident in his expression, was a gut-wrenching blow, leaving me devastated. I tried to rationalize, reminding myself of his other children, yet it did little to soothe the ache in my heart."

Questioning Divine Care in Times of Trial

After realizing the consequences of being unequally yoked with CW, I grappled with a profound sense of overwhelm.

My cries to the Lord were laden with confusion and distress: 'Lord, do You not see my suffering? Are You indifferent to the treatment I'm enduring?' This bitterness stemmed from feeling unfairly treated. Marrying CW wasn't a conscious defiance of God's will; I believed it was endorsed through what I perceived as a divine sign.".

Proverbs 19:3 in the ESV Bible reflects a hard truth: "When a man's folly brings his way to ruin, his heart rages against the LORD." This verse resonated deeply with me, teaching that if a supposed sign contradicts God's Word, it cannot be from Him. Even sincere intentions, if they violate God's teachings, lead to adverse consequences.

Journey from Spiritual Strife to Renewal

For months, I was engulfed in bitterness, resentment, and anger due to my husband's rejection and what I perceived as God's silence, coupled with unmet expectations in my marriage.

At that stage in my relationship with Jesus, embracing His teachings of love, forgiveness, and patience seemed beyond my reach. I found myself drawn to the seductive allure of bitterness, resentment, and anger—Satan's sweets—rather than partaking in Christ's humble pie of love and forgiveness.

These toxic emotions clogged my spiritual pores, hindering my growth and connection with Jesus. This blockage led to a significant spiritual setback, akin to a heart attack in spiritual terms, which led to me backsliding.

Embracing the Transformative Power of God's Grace

After a period of spiritual desertion, I was in a state of despair. But then, God's grace, a beacon of hope, stirred my heart, compelling me to pray and repent. I asked to be renewed into fellowship, a journey that echoes the prodigal son's return in Luke 15.

This led to a pivotal moment of repentance and a heartfelt plea to God for forgiveness and guidance in discipleship and love.

My inspiration came from Jonah's acknowledgment of God's grace and nature—compassionate, merciful, and forgiving (Jonah 4:2).

As I reached out for His help, I felt a gentle breeze of the Holy Spirit, gradually cleansing my heart of bitterness, resentment, and anger. This cleansing enabled me to grow in obedience and love, a transformation I could never have achieved on my own.

As you navigate the complexities of your unequally yoked marriage, I urge you to trust in God's grace wholeheartedly. This trust will empower you to fulfill the role envisioned by God for you as a spouse in such a union, a role that is unattainable without leaning on the grace He provides.

It's crucial to recognize that you are not the savior of your unbelieving spouse; that role belongs uniquely to God. You must understand and accept your righteousness like a filthy rag in God's sight.

Embrace these humbling truths, which will steer you toward relying entirely on God's grace, which enables you to thrive and radiate His love and light from within.

Our life choices are mirrors, reflecting our wisdom or folly.

CHAPTER 3

Understanding God's Mariage Plan

A Journey of Faith and Understanding

After rejuvenating my faith, I was drawn to sit at Jesus' feet and bask in His teachings daily, especially once I committed to walking His path.

My aspirations were for CW to embrace Christianity and live happily ever after. I wholeheartedly adopted the role of a devoted wife, nurturing the hope that CW would mirror my gestures of love.

Yet, seeking warmth and tenderness from him outside intimate moments felt akin to attempting to extract a tooth barehanded.

The dream of him finding salvation and becoming my king, leading us into a fairytale ending, began to fade. Our relationship felt adversarial.

The lingering question was why we couldn't synergize our efforts. The divine blueprint for marital bliss explained why.

God's Design for Marriage

God designed marriage to be a sacred covenant between a man and a woman. It must be a lifelong commitment, a union in which they become one flesh, and a foundation for procreation and raising children. God's desire for marriage often focuses on intimacy, spiritual growth, mutual self-sacrifice, commitment, faithfulness, and pursuing God's will within the marriage relationship.

This sacred covenant occurs when two individuals become one in Christ Jesus. When the two become one, they love, submit, and respect each other according to God's decrees.

Even in an unequally yoked marriage between a believer in Christ and a non-believer, God honors this as a covenantal union because they vow their marriage before Him. Therefore, the command to love and respect applies just as much. However, the unbelieving spouse will not understand or accept this as a spiritual union.

Diamonds Under Pressure: The Paradox of Unity and Division in Marriage

In the profound depths of the Earth, under extreme pressure and temperature, carbon atoms are meticulously aligned to form the unbreakable bonds of a diamond. This offering is a rich metaphor for the journey of a couple striving toward unity in marriage.

This analogy encapsulates the essence of a relationship fortified through adversity, where challenges act not as forces of division but as catalysts for growth, drawing parallels to a couple united in purpose and understanding.

The transformation into a diamond symbolizes the potential for trials and tribulations to deepen the connection between partners, turning individual flaws into a collective strength that is both resilient and beautiful.

However, when considering an unequally yoked marriage, where foundational beliefs and aspirations diverge, the diamond formation analogy takes a starkly different turn.

Instead of the pressure solidifying a unified front, it may exacerbate the fissures between the partners, reflecting the warnings in Joshua 23:12-13 and 2 Corinthians 6:14-15.

These scriptures caution against the inherent instability and discord that will arise from profound disparities in core values and beliefs within a marriage.

In such unions, the intense pressures of life do not lead to the creation of a diamond but rather threaten the integrity of the relationship, suggesting that without a shared foundation, the forces meant to unite lead to fragmentation and disunity.

This divergence in outcomes underscores the critical importance of compatibility and shared convictions in navigating the pressures of life together.

To build a healthy marriage, God has given us clear guidelines. One explicitly stated rule is not to marry an unbeliever. He refers to this as unequal yoking. Joshua 23:12–13 (ESV) details the consequences if a believer marries an unbeliever.

"They shall be snares and traps for you, whips on your sides, and thorns in your eyes until you perish from this good ground the Lord God has given you."

The New Testament warns us not to marry an unbeliever. According to 2 Corinthians 6:14-15, (ESV)."Do not be unequally yoked with unbelievers.

For what partnership does righteousness have with lawlessness? Or what fellowship does light have with darkness? What accord does Christ have with Belial? Or what portion will a believer share with an unbeliever?"

These Scriptures emphasize the challenges of marrying an unbeliever, often called "unequal yoking."

What Is an Unequally Yoked Marriage?

Before we begin, let's explore the structure of a physical yoke. It's a wooden beam used to unite two animals, such as oxen, to pull a plow or a cart.

The purpose of the yoke is to ensure that the animals work together in harmony, with each pulling an equal amount of weight and moving in the same direction.

In the Bible, the term" yoke" is often associated with slavery, bondage, and hardship, such as when the children of Israel were under the yoke of Pharaoh (Exodus 1, 1 Kings 12:4, Jeremiah 27:8).

The term "unequally yoked" comes from the Bible, specifically from 2 Corinthians 6:14, where the apostle Paul warns:" Do not be unequally yoked with unbelievers. The Greek verb *heterozygeo,* which means "*unequally yoked,*" means to come under another of a different sort."

Here, it is used metaphorically in the sense of" to have fellowship with one who is not spiritual equal" (Thayer, p. 254).

An unequally yoked marriage occurs when a person who has become born again, upon confessing Christ's expiatory death for their sins and receiving a regenerated nature through the Holy Spirit, marries someone who has not accepted Christ's expiatory death for their sins and has not experienced the same spiritual transformation.

This marriage creates a union between two individuals with different spiritual natures, leading to an unequally yoked marriage.

Can an unbeliever and a believer achieve spiritual unity in marriage, given the importance of understanding what it means to be 'born again'?

Understanding the Difference Between Abuse and Persecution in Marriage

An abusive marriage and persecution both represent forms of oppression, yet they differ significantly in scope and nature. An abusive marriage involves a personal relationship where one partner exerts control through violence, manipulation, or coercion, leading to a significant power imbalance that can profoundly affect the victim's health and stability. Notably, the Bible condemns such abuse, and those suffering are encouraged to get out and seek safety. Conversely, persecution can serve as a means through which God refines and strengthens His followers. Unlike abuse, persecution is associated with suffering for one's faith—this might include emotional isolation, rejection, criticism, ridicule, and other trials related to standing firm in one's faith convictions. These challenges test the believer's character and patience, often strengthening their dependence on God.

Although I have never experienced abuse in my marriage, I have encountered all the trials above of persecution. These were daunting challenges, yet God's grace refined my faith and bolstered my spiritual resilience through them. Peter likens such trials to gold refined in fire, which tests our faith and produces perseverance and maturity.

Understanding the distinction between abuse and persecution is crucial in a marriage. God unequivocally condemns abuse, but He allows persecution as a tool to mature and refine our spirits.

By embracing faith, engaging in prayer, loving God wholeheartedly, letting the Word of God renew our minds, surrendering our desires, and loving ourselves with the love that comes from God, we can emerge from these trials stronger, wiser, and more deeply aligned with God's divine purposes.

Unbelievers: Who Are They?

An unbeliever is someone who has not accepted Jesus as their Lord and Savior and does not believe in Jesus' death as the propitiation for sin.

Therefore, their sins have not been forgiven and cleansed by Jesus' blood.

An unbeliever does not have God's nature in them because they have not been born of the Holy Spirit and do not follow Christ's teachings (John 3:3-5; Matthew 11:28-30; Romans 8:9–10; 1 John 3:9; Matthew 7:24-27).

An unbeliever is someone who has not taken on Christ's yoke when Jesus issues this invitation to all,

"Take my yoke upon you and learn from me, for I am gentle and humble in heart, and you will find rest for your souls. For my yoke is easy, and my burden is light" (Matthew 11:29-30 NIV).

Suppose you and your spouse identify as believers, but you sense that your relationship is unequally yoked. In this case, it leads to a crucial question: Can two believers be unequally yoked?

From a biblical perspective, when considering the concept of spiritual rebirth, as explained above (2 Corinthians 6:14), two born-again believers cannot be regarded as "unequally yoked."

However, it's important to note that differences in their spiritual maturity are significant. In the spiritual journey described by Paul in Romans 14, two believers are distinguished by their varying maturity; one is considered the weaker Christian. Varying maturity is likened to a powerful analogy.

Imagine a young, untrained ox yoked alongside an older, experienced one. This pairing is not just a matter of harnessing two animals with the exact nature; it's a profound lesson in growth and guidance. The younger ox, initially inexperienced and perhaps unsteady, gradually learns from the steady pace and wisdom of the older.

This process isn't swift, but the younger ox adapts over time, aligning its steps with its companion. The transformation is subtle yet profound. These oxen are not unequally yoked because they are of the same kind.

How might Romans 14 be used to understand the dynamic of believers of varying maturity levels?

Hebrews 5:13-14 uses the metaphor of milk and solid food to encourage believers to grow in their faith, moving from a basic understanding of Christian principles to a more mature, nuanced, and discerning grasp of their faith, especially in ethical and moral decision-making.

To fully grasp spiritual growth, it's essential to understand that human beings are composed of three distinct parts: Spirit, soul, and body, as mentioned in 1 Thessalonians 5:23.

In this tripartite structure, only the spirit undergoes regeneration or rebirth. On the other hand, the soul, essentially our mind, does not experience this transformation.

Our flesh is not subject to rebirth and will continually conflict with our renewed spiritual self. This persistent battle emphasizes the crucial role of renewing our minds in fostering spiritual growth.

The state of our mind determines whether we are led by our spiritual self or swayed by our physical desires.

It is a transformative journey to renew our minds with the Word of God, the Bible. This concept of renewing the mind is critically underscored in Romans 12:2 and 1 Peter 2:2.

Without this renewal, the old nature, influenced by worldly desires and thoughts, remains predominant, hindering spiritual growth.

A believer must actively work on renewing their mind to grow spiritually and to walk in alignment with the Holy Spirit.

If one believer is actively renewing their mind and dying to self and the other isn't, one will be more mature than the other. 1 Corinthians 3:1-3

As Matthew 7:21 points out, there are cases where someone may profess faith without genuinely embodying it.

This distinction is crucial, underscoring that mere verbal acknowledgment of faith is not the same as the transformative journey of spiritual growth that involves both the Spirit and the renewal of the mind.

If this is the scenario, they are spiritually unequally yoked because one needs to undergo the authentic 'born again' experience.

Can you perceive how a supposedly equally yoked marriage might face similar challenges as an unequally yoked one if one partner is spiritually mature while the other is not?

CHAPTER 4

Contemplating Divorce in a Strained Marriage

Once I grasped God's blueprint for marriage, the reasons behind the chasm between CW and me became stark. Our spiritual mismatch, with me being saved and him not, was a glaring reality.

Our roles in the relationship were also at odds, with me being the pursuer and him the distancer.

These fundamental disparities in our spiritual beliefs and relational dynamics were clear signs that our paths were diverging, not converging into a harmonious, God-centered union.

A preacher once stated, "Marrying an unbeliever diverts you from your God-ordained path."

This sermon struck a chord with me, as all my efforts to win CW's love seemed futile. Each time I reached out for his emotional connection, he seemed to withdraw. My response to this emotional distance was often anger, leading me to consider divorce whenever our disagreements escalated.

This pattern persisted for years. Reflecting on this, I now realize how my actions contributed to the erosion of our relationship. The pain and strain I caused were not fleeting but deeply affected his emotions and trust.

Convinced by the preacher's words that this marriage was a deviation from my divine path, I contemplated divorce to realign with my destiny. Our marriage left me questioning how I could continue in a marriage where I had missed my destiny. "God, had I missed Your plan by marrying CW, as the preacher said?"

Revolutionized

The answer to my question came from a book called *Lord, I Want to Know You* by Kay Arthur, which discusses God's names and how they relate to our daily lives. One of God's names is El Elyon, Most High God, Sovereign Ruler. El Elyon is a name that designates God as the sovereign ruler of the universe (Job 2:1-4, Genesis 14:18–20).

Nothing happens in this world without His approval. Mrs. Arthur noted in her book that God knew what would happen in this world before it did, and nothing happens without God's permission (Genesis 20:6).

I came to understand that my marriage required God's approval before it could proceed. Knowing that God had sanctioned my marriage reassured me that I was following my destined path, not missing it as the preacher suggested. This realization brought me great joy and a renewed sense of hope.

With an understanding of God as El Elyon, the God Most High and Sovereign Ruler, I had a paradigm shift about my unequally yoked marriage. God had permitted my marriage. With this new understanding, I consulted the Bible about the roles of wife and husband.

Roles of the Husband

Husbands, love your wives, even as Christ also loved the church, and gave himself for it; .... So ought men to love their wives as their own bodies. He that loveth his wife loveth himself. For no man ever yet hated his own flesh; but nourisheth and cherisheth it, even as the Lord the church:

The husband is called to be the head of his wife and to cherish his wife as his own body, nurturing and cherishing her as Christ loves His church and to live with her by knowledge (Ephesians 5:23, 25, 28–29; 1 Peter 3:7).

Roles of the Wife

Submitting yourselves one to another in the fear of God. Wives, submit yourselves unto your own husbands, as unto the Lord. For the husband is the head of the wife, even as Christ is the head of the church: .... the wife see that she reverence her husband.

Wives are called to submit to their husbands as unto the Lord. They must respect and submit to their husbands' leadership and honor him by allowing their will to fall under his. If the husband and wife differ on an issue, the wife supports him by following his lead (unless it would be a sin to do so) and not usurping his authority (Ephesians 5:22, 33).

Now, let's look at a fuller context of marriage regarding positions and roles.

Ephesians 5:21-24, 33 (KJV):

Submitting yourselves one to another in the fear of God. Wives, submit yourselves unto your own husbands, as unto the Lord. For the husband is the head of the wife, even as Christ is the head of the church: and he is the savior of the body. Therefore, as the church is subject unto Christ, so let the wives be to their own husbands in everything ... Nevertheless, let every one of you in particular so love his wife even as himself... even as the Lord the church.... the wife see that she reverence her husband. Who [Jesus], being in the form of God, thought it not robbery to be equal with God: But made himself of no reputation, and took upon him the form of a servant, and was made in the likeness of men ... (emphasis added)

This means that Christ was an equal member of the triune God, but He submitted to the authority of the Father for the sake of order. In the same way, man and woman are equal before God. Still, the man is positioned to have authority in the relationship, and the woman sees submission to his leadership as a blessing.

But what happens when this unity is stopped by an unbeliever's inability to understand the concept of sacrificial love, as Christ did for His church?

An unbelieving husband lacks God's Spirit to guide him in loving his wife with the depth and selflessness that the scriptures demand.

This gap in understanding often escalates, leading to a cycle of frustration, anger, and bitterness, as he feels pressured and judged, unable to meet the expectations of his Christian wife. Similarly, an unbelieving wife struggles to embrace the role scripture assigns to her. The concept of submitting to her husband, as unto the Lord, is obscured by spiritual blindness. The biblical call to submission will seem nonsensical to her in a world where such teachings are often viewed as outdated or oppressive.

After comprehending my role as a wife, I retrieved my wedding license, holding it before God; I pledged to Him that I would love CW as He loved him. Then I reiterated my wedding vows, vowing to God, "I take CW to be my wedded husband. To have and to hold from this day forward.

For better, for worse, for richer, for poorer. In sickness and health, to love and cherish till death do us part. I added, whether content or discontent in my marriage, I will remain until death do us part. Or until he violates the marriage covenant by infidelity or deserting the marriage physically." I also removed divorce from my vocabulary in this commitment.

I affirmed my commitment when I shared my renewed commitment to our marriage to CW. I intertwined my fingers behind my back, a physical symbol of my bond. Then, turning my back toward him, "I am bound to this marriage as my fingers are bonded," I told him, happy or unhappy, "until death or unless you break our covenant, do us apart."

However, his blank, silent response left me feeling disheartened and questioning the impact of my words. I felt like a fool telling him about my new commitment to our marriage.

I became angry; I retracted my vow to God, but I couldn't retract it; it was a sacred promise to God, and I was reminded of the scriptures emphasizing the seriousness of such a vow.

Deuteronomy 23:21 and Numbers 30:2 stress the importance of fulfilling vows made to God. They highlight the gravity of commitments made to God, and the expectation of their fulfillment, reminds us of the seriousness with which God views our promises to Him.

In the New Testament, Jesus counsels against making vows in Matthew 5:33-37. Jesus advises against swearing oaths and instead recommends a straightforward approach to communication.

He emphasizes the value of direct and honest communication, advising against the complexities and potential pitfalls of oath-making. Please, do not promise to God because He will demand it of you!

Unveiling the Purpose: Understanding God's Reason for Allowing My Unequally Yoked Marriage

The revelation that God allowed my marriage didn't change the dynamics until I discovered the purpose of why God sanctioned my marriage.

One day, as I was sitting at Christ's feet, I read Romans chapter 8:29–30 (NASB20), which says,

For those whom He foreknew, He also predestined to become conformed to the image of His Son, so that He would be the firstborn among many brothers and sisters; and these whom He predestined,

He also called; and these whom He called, He also justified; and these whom He justified, He also glorified.

As I contemplated those scriptural passages, I saw why God had permitted CW and me to marry to conform me to Jesus's image. CW was part of God's plan for my spiritual development. His habit of emotionally distancing himself during disagreements manifested my struggles with anger, impatience, and a failure to be quiet.

These attributes were not in line with the loving nature of Christ. This awareness acted as a divine tool, steering me towards nurturing more patience and genuine love, thereby gradually transforming me to reflect on Jesus's characteristics in my daily actions.

Every test of responding with gentleness instead of annoyance was a step in my spiritual conformity to Christ's image. I realized that these lessons would keep presenting themselves until I had truly learned and grown from them, finally passing them. My process of learning and adjusting to these teachings was admittedly a slow one.

I gained hope for my unequally yoked marriage as I developed a deeper understanding of God's purpose for my marriage. I no longer thought I had missed my destiny, as that preacher said I had.

Before grasping the divine purpose for my marriage, I was akin to a frog seated in a pot of cold water on the stove, gradually heating to a boil, unknowingly succumbing to regret and frustration. I was a poor example of a wife and a witness to Christ.

For instance, I often disregarded my husband's feelings, prioritizing my needs over his, much like the woman in Proverbs 14:1b, who was tearing down her house with her hands.

Unbeknownst to me, my actions and decisions eroded the foundation of our home and marriage. I was quick to criticize and slow to listen, creating an environment of tension rather than one of understanding and support.

Yet, even during this period of unwitting self-destruction, God's care remained constant and tender, resembling how a mother gently cared for her newborn.

His love was a steady source of strength, sustaining me even when I strayed in ignorance or defiance. In those times, His mercy was a cleansing balm, washing away my missteps and clothing me in renewed faith.

Yet, every time I faltered, God's grace was there to catch me, a testament to His unwavering mercy. His love carried me, offering solace and reassurance in moments of doubt and weakness.

As a result, God stepped back; it was time for Him to wean me since I understood the basic rules. I had arrived at a pivotal moment when maturing and paying the cost of discipleship was essential.

The two most significant days in your life are the day you experience rebirth and the day you understand why God chose to save you.

CHAPTER 5

Discerning God's Voice

My journey of discerning God's voice has been transformative, leading me from confusion and doubt to profound spiritual growth. It's about honing the ability to recognize His guidance amidst the chaos and distractions of everyday life.

This process, which involves patience, prayer, and immersion in scripture, has heightened my awareness of God's guidance.

Over time, this discernment has enabled me to make decisions that align with divine wisdom and not signs, enhancing my faith and deepening my relationship with God. It's a continuous, life-enhancing process that brings clarity and purpose to my spiritual walk.

While learning to discern God's voice, the Gospel of John, particularly the verse, "My sheep hear my voice, and I know them, and they follow me" (John 10:27), provides a profound insight into our relationship with Jesus. This verse beautifully illustrates the intimate connection between Christ and His followers, emphasizing that His true followers are not just attuned to His voice but guided by His words, fostering a sense of closeness and belonging in His divine presence.

Understanding How God Communicates

Hearing Jesus' voice as His sheep is communicated through His Words. It's not just about developing sensitivity to the spiritual guidance and promptings that come through the Holy Spirit. It's about fostering a deep, personal relationship with Jesus, where His words and teachings communicate His guidance for our decisions and actions.

This discernment is not about audible sounds but Scripture, prayer, the Holy Spirit, community, life's circumstances, and the natural world. Each offers unique insights and guidance for navigating an inner knowing and understanding that guides us by God's will and Word, creating a sense of intimacy and closeness with our Savior.

The Role of Scripture and Prayer in Discernment

Discernment is essential for making decisions that align with God's will. Scripture and prayer are critical pillars in this process. They also provide the necessary guidance and tools for understanding God's intentions, instilling a sense of direction and purpose in our spiritual journey. Scripture is central to discernment, offering principles, narratives, commands, and wisdom to guide believers in every aspect of life.

Prayer, a sacred and personal connection with God, is not just a tool but a direct line to Him. It allows you to seek His guidance and confirmation, asking for wisdom and understanding of His will.

This direct communication makes your decisions more secure and aligned with His divine plan. Adequate discernment involves an ongoing dialogue between scripture and prayer, aligning personal desires with divine wisdom.

It's important to note that individual desires are not inherently wrong but may not always align with God's will.

Scripture and prayer equip believers to discern the difference and make decisions that reflect a deep understanding of God's Word and attunement to His Spirit.

The Pitfalls of Seeking Signs

My request for a divine sign misled me. Lord," I prayed, "if CW is divorced, I'll take this as my sign from You to marry CW. Well, I got that sign, and after marrying CW, I realized it contradicted God's teachings.

This realization underscored the importance of seeking wisdom through scripture and godly counsel rather than searching for signs and leaning on your understanding. Stay in line with Jesus's teaching that faith, not signs, should guide our actions.

Even after that incident in the early years of my marriage, I was overwhelmed with a sense of hopelessness about my marriage.

A compelling internal voice suggested that I had endured enough, and it was time to break free. This idea was supported by what I recalled from 1 Corinthians 7 about possibly leaving a marriage without seeking another union. Seeking clarity and desperate for guidance, I prayed earnestly to God. Bolstered by the urge for a divine sign, I turned on a Christian broadcast, hoping it would provide clarity and direction.

My prayer was miraculously answered when a preacher proclaimed a message of liberation. "It is time for your liberation from bondage," the preacher declared, "this year is a new beginning, leaving behind the past and looking towards abundance in this New Year."

This divine message filled me with amazement. I celebrated this apparent sign from God that He was liberating me from my marriage.

However, my celebration was short-lived; as I returned to the living room, another message from a different preacher boomed from the television: "God says to be still and know I am God. Don't you leave that marriage," as the preacher pointed his hands toward me!

I stood in awe, speechless.

Challenges in Discernment

The stark contrast in these messages left me bewildered and questioning. How could God send such conflicting guidance? The challenge of discernment was overwhelming, and I felt lost in it. Amid the confusion, I focused on prayer to discover what was happening. Gradually, the confusion began to clear. The lessons I gained weren't solely about my marriage but about seeking a harmonious relationship between divine will and my discernment. I understood that even when messages appear contradictory, they can each carry wisdom that guides us to a higher understanding of ourselves. In the wake of that incident, I began to ask myself deep questions and examine my feelings more critically. What did I truly want, and what was my heart telling me beyond the immediate emotions?

Was I seeking liberation because it was the best path forward, or was I running away from challenges that, if faced, could lead to growth? These questions opened the door to a level of introspection that I'd never ventured into before.

For example, I questioned why I felt such an urgent need to leave. Was it genuinely because my marriage was irreparably broken, or was I holding onto old wounds and fears that prevented me from carrying my cross? Sitting with these questions and reflecting on them, I acknowledged how my past experiences and disappointments had shaped my perspective on relationships and commitment.

It struck me that specific old patterns and defense mechanisms I clung to obstructed my ability to foster connections, and this moment of clarity highlighted the necessity of addressing personal issues before considering the end of a relationship.

'Personal growth' is a process of self-improvement and self-discovery.

It involves recognizing and addressing our shortcomings and allowing the mending power of the Holy Spirit to mend us to become Christ-like. I realized that my yearning for liberation was not inherently misguided, but I needed first to turn inward and ensure I wasn't simply evading the discomfort of personal growth. This introspection made me understand that I needed to confront my issues, shortcomings, and unresolved sins before contemplating the end of the relationship;

otherwise, I would carry these same burdens into any future relationship.

Exploring feelings and motivations was a pivotal step in my journey. It illuminated the crucial difference between God's Voice and impulsive reaction, a distinction that empowered me to navigate life's challenges with greater clarity and wisdom. I discovered that while some situations demand decisive action, others require patience and deep reflection, a realization that has guided my decisions ever since.

Understanding the Difference Between Signs and Confirmation

In the Bible, signs often refer to miraculous events or wonders that manifest God's power and authority. However, repeatedly, the Scriptures caution against relying solely on signs for faith. Seeking signs is often about wanting proof for the sake of evidence, which can lead to a shallow faith that wavers when the miraculous is absent. In contrast, seeking confirmation is a mature approach that involves discerning God's will through spiritual practices and trusting in His providence and timing.

Now, I find myself in prayerful reflection, weighing these conflicting messages and striving to discern the path that aligns with God's will for my life.

I also realized my struggle was not with God's clarity but my spiritual immaturity. I was still a novice in my faith, not yet adept at understanding the nuanced ways God communicated with me.

This revelation underscored the paramount importance of cultivating spiritual discernment. In a world filled with competing voices and conflicting ideologies, this discernment becomes a powerful tool for navigating life's complexities and making decisions that align with God's will.

Recognizing God's Voice

Discerning God's voice from one's thoughts or desires is essential. 1 John 4:1 advises, "Dear friends, do not believe every spirit, but test the spirits to see whether they are from God."

This highlights the importance of testing personal impressions against Scripture and the wise counsel of spiritually mature individuals. To develop the ability to hear Jesus' voice, consider the following practices:

- **Engage deeply with the word of God through systematic Bible study and apply biblical truths to life's decisions.**
- **Develop a robust prayer life for direct communication with God, guided by Philippians 4:6-7.**
- **Nurture sensitivity to the Holy Spirit, who guides into all truth (John 16:13)."**
- **Do not lean on your understanding. (Proverbs 3:5)**

By integrating these practices into daily life, we can cultivate a more profound sensitivity to hearing Jesus' voice, ensuring His wisdom and truth guide our spiritual walk. Our relationship with Jesus, marked by continuous listening and following, is central to living in tune with Him.

How can you discern God's guidance more effectively in decisions not explicitly addressed in the scriptures?

CHAPTER 6

The Price of Transformation

The Awakening

"Forget you!" I screamed, "My voice was trembling with a mix of anger and hurt as CW strode towards the door, his departure for yet another night of partying feeling like a betrayal. "You make me sick!"

The words erupted from me, raw and unfiltered, and I hurled a shoe at him in a moment of impulsive rage. It whizzed through the air, representing all the pent-up frustration that I had been bottling up inside, missing him by a mere inch as he coolly shut the door behind him, leaving me with the echo of my outburst.

After my commitment to Jesus, CW started frequenting the club as if to distance himself from my newfound faith. In moments of frustration, I accused him of being uncaring, a reflection of the silent, growing divide that was emerging between us.

I tried to envision his perspective and his coping mechanism against the drastic change in his wife. Was he seeking solace, or was this a silent protest against my newfound path? The uncertainty gnawed at me, leaving a void filled only by my assumptions.

As I sat alone, the house echoed with the ghosts of laughter, the clink of glasses, the rhythm of dances, and the smiling glances I imagined CW partaking in. My heart was a battleground of emotions.

Anger and jealousy surged through me, intensified by the quiet of our home. Our once-shared dreams and laughter had faded into a stark contrast of beliefs. His absence tonight was a tangible reminder of the growing distance between us.

I thought of our early days before my spiritual conversion and how we navigated our differences by discussing things. But now, as his world drifted further from mine, I felt more isolated in my faith. Sleep was elusive, and focus seemed impossible to grasp. I turned to prayer and the Bible, hoping to find respite from the storm inside me. However, my negative thoughts were relentless.

They overpowered me, making it impossible to heed Paul's advice in 2 Corinthians 10:5 about casting down imaginations and bringing every thought into obedience to Christ.

Despite my earnest attempts, I struggled to reign in my runaway emotions and thoughts, unable to utilize Christ's authority to put my thoughts into obedience.

As CW opened the door after 1:30 am, it was a habit of mine to feign sleep. This silent act of mine was a veil, a way to mask the turmoil within. Come morning, my behavior towards him was distant and frosty.

I moved around our apartment with an unmistakable air of resentment, a visible burden borne from my lingering thoughts about him possibly being in the company of another woman.

These unvoiced but deeply felt thoughts cast shadows over our interactions, coloring them with the hues of my internal struggle.

Encounter with Mother Hodge

It was amidst this strife that Mother Hodge entered my life. A revered figure in our church, her soulful songs and rhythmic cymbal playing were a balm to my troubled spirit. Despite never having experienced infidelity in my marriage like Mother Hodge, her story deeply resonated with me.

The Price of Discipleship

This encounter with Mother Hodge made me ponder the actual cost of discipleship.

The price of discipleship, a concept I had embraced in theory, now loomed over me like a mountain I was unprepared to climb.

It dawned on me that the journey of faith was more than just accepting salvation; it was an ongoing battle to align every thought and every action with Christ's teachings.

This battle was spiritual and deeply personal, testing the foundations of who I was and aspired to be in His light.

Path to Spiritual Maturity"

As dawn broke, casting a soft glow in the kitchen, I reflected on Mother Hodge's profound peace and teachings, which gave me a deeper understanding of the spiritual journey to walk in Christ's authority. This personal journey of understanding the spiritual path revealed that while salvation is a precious gift freely bestowed by God, truly living out our spiritual inheritance and the abundant life promised in Christ required paying the cost of discipleship to use Christ's authority and to achieve personal transformation into Christ's image.

The story of the Israelites, who were given a land flowing with milk and honey—a symbol of divine abundance, resonates with this concept.

They didn't just receive the land; they had to put in the effort and dedication to cultivate it and enjoy its richness. Similarly, to truly experience Jesus's spiritual riches, we must wholeheartedly embrace the cost of discipleship. Jesus articulates this cost in Luke 9:23: "If any man will come after me, let him deny himself, and take up his cross, and follow Me."

In Luke 14:26, He further states: "And hate not his father, and mother, and wife, and children, and brethren, and sisters, yea, and his own life also, he cannot be my disciple."

The message was clear, yet its weight felt immense. Genuinely following Christ meant more than verbal commitment; it required paying the cost of discipleship. This challenge demanded respect and admiration, as it was the path to personal transformation into Christ's image.

Let's review the costs associated with each aspect of discipleship Christ mentioned, reflecting on the depth and implications of such a commitment.

Come After Me, Cost: A ceaseless pursuit, a daily decision demanding unwavering personal commitment and deliberate intent. This payment requires individual responsibility and intentionality.

A pathway laid out by Jesus—following in His footsteps, is not merely about adhering to a set of doctrines or moral codes but about developing a personal relationship with Him as the leader and Lord of your life.

It calls you into a profound personal connection with Him, acknowledging Him as the guide and sovereign of your existence.

Deny yourself," comes the directive. The price? A perpetual self-emptying, a relinquishing of all autonomy. This act of self-denial is a surrender of one's control, desires, and will to the divine. It is a deliberate choice to let ego-driven desires no longer steer one's course but to harmonize one's will with God's.

It beckons one to forsake selfish ambitions, pride, and ego in favor of a life devoted to serving God and others.

The cross" resonates as a testament to the profound cost involved: an unending, day-to-day commitment to embrace hardship, withstand opposition, suffer persecution, endure insults, overcome lack, navigate trials, and, if it comes to it, face death itself—all in the Name of Christ.

"Follow me," The price? A relentless, unceasing endeavor to emulate the example and teachings of Jesus.

It demands an ongoing act of renunciation of one's self-centered desires, alongside a willing acceptance of the distinct challenges and burdens accompanying a life of faith.

This path is a profound transformation to mirror Christ's Characteristics and likeness in every facet of one's existence.

"Love me," The Cost? Total and unconditional commitment. Loving Jesus above all else means that allegiance to Him supersedes all other relationships and personal considerations.

It encompasses loving God with all one's heart, soul, mind, and strength, indicating a level of devotion that includes the entirety of one's being.

I realized then why I couldn't put my untamed thoughts as they ran wild into the obedience of Christ. I had embraced the gift of salvation but had yet to fully understand and pay the cost of discipleship.

This cost wasn't financial nor about self-righteousness but a matter of the heart and soul.

In those quiet, reflective moments, it became evident that I had first to walk the difficult path of discipleship to wield Christ's authority in my life.

It was a path of self-denial, carrying my cross through trials and tribulations and reshaping my life to mirror His image. This was the price - a relentless, unwavering devotion to His teachings and way of life.

With the morning light still lingering, a newfound clarity crystallized within me. Spiritual growth, I realized, was the key to unlocking the true essence of discipleship. It wasn't an overnight transformation but a journey that involved unwavering faith, dedicated prayer, and an all-consuming love for God.

This growth demanded more than passive belief; it required active engagement with God's Word, letting it seep into every corner of my life and guide my actions and decisions. It called for self-death—relinquishing my desires and ego—to be reborn in Christ's love and compassion.

I understood that loving myself as Christ loves us was integral to this journey. It meant treating myself with kindness and forgiveness, recognizing my worth in God's eyes, and using this as a foundation to extend the same love and grace to CW and others.

The path to spiritual maturity was clear yet daunting. But the peace of living in harmony with God's reassured me. Paying the cost of discipleship was indeed a challenge, but one that promised a life of deeper meaning and purpose rooted in the love and teachings of Christ.

From Believer to Disciple

Reflecting further, I understood that my relationship with Christ was like that of a believer who accepts and acknowledges but does not fully dive into the teachings or embody the lifestyle.

As a believer, I was still in control, choosing when and how to incorporate obedience into my life.

But now, I yearned for a deeper connection — that of a disciple. A disciple sees Jesus not just as a figure to be revered but as Adonai, Lord, and Master, guiding every aspect of their life. The shift from believer to disciple isn't just in title but in the essence of one's being and actions.

As a disciple, it was no longer about merely believing in Christ's teachings but molding my life to reflect them. This transformation meant working the power within me, the Holy Spirit, to apply Christ's authority in every circumstance, aligning my actions, thoughts, and decisions with His will.

It was a commitment to active spiritual growth, a continuous learning process, adapting, dying to myself, and evolving to become more Christ-like.

This understanding shed light on my struggles. To navigate life's complexities and challenges as a disciple, I needed to embrace this more profound commitment, allowing Jesus to be the true master of my life, guiding me through trials and triumphs.

My resolve to follow this path of discipleship was met with internal and external opposition. But Mother Hodge's story served as a reminder that the faith journey involves navigating such challenges with grace and forgiveness.

With my resolve to transition from believer to disciple, I dedicated time each day to sit at Christ's feet, metaphorically speaking.

Sitting at Christ's feet was a time to understand my role in God's kingdom. However, this path was not without obstacles, reminiscent of Mary's challenges in Luke 10:40.

As Mary, Lazarus's sister, embarked on her spiritual journey, she encountered significant challenges, primarily from her sister Martha. These challenges, detailed in Luke 10:40, took various forms to hinder Mary's path to spiritual growth.

Mary's story illustrates our opposition to pursuing spiritual depth. As I walked this path, I identified four distinct challenges that reflected Mary's experiences, each threatening her spiritual development.

Luke 10:40. "Lord, dost thou not care that my sister hath left me to serve alone? Bid her therefore that she helps me."

Complaint

The initial hurdle Mary faced was Martha's complaint. Mary, absorbed in Jesus' teachings and seeking to understand her role in God's kingdom, was at the receiving end of Martha's complaint, centered around Mary not assisting in the kitchen. This scenario reflects a broader truth: choosing to learn from Christ will attract criticism.

My personal experience resonates with this. When I dedicated an hour daily to Bible study, my family's reactions were mixed. My children questioned my availability, and my husband remarked on my constant engagement with the Bible. These complaints are not mere coincidences; they are distractions that divert attention from spiritual pursuits.

When you commit to learning from Christ, like dedicating time to studying God's Word, it's common to face complaints from those around you.

Remember, the real issue is not having limited time but making conscious choices.

Opposition, such as complaints about your dedication, often means you're on the right spiritual track. Embrace these challenges as affirmations of your commitment to your faith.

False Accusations

The second challenge involves accusations. Martha accused Mary of neglecting her responsibilities, a claim far from Mary's intention of learning about discipleship. This mirrors a universal experience for those deeply engaged in seeking God. I, too, faced similar accusations questioning my motives behind studying the Bible and attending Bible Study.

Such experiences are hurtful, yet they're a testament to your commitment. Matthew 5:11 reminds us of the blessedness of being wrongly accused for righteousness' sake. Defending your intentions is less important than recognizing the honor in such accusations.

Being Misunderstood

Misunderstanding is another obstacle. Martha misinterpreted Mary's intentions, seeing neglect where there was a desire for spiritual learning. I've experienced similar misunderstandings, like when a fellow church member initially perceived my enthusiastic worship as showmanship. Explaining that my worship was an expression of gratitude for salvation, I realized that such misunderstandings shouldn't be taken personally. They are often another tactic to create spiritual offense.

Adverse Actions

Finally, Mary faced direct opposition through Martha's plea to Jesus for intervention. This kind of adverse action is common for those deeply committed to their faith. I faced a similar issue with my manager. She summoned me to her office to inform me that several colleagues had expressed discomfort with my habit of blessing God/Jesus's name in response to their casual or disrespectful mentions of it in the workplace.

I was accused of being irritating, which placed me at a crossroads: either ceasing my blessing of God's sacred name or standing firmly by it. I chose to uphold my practice, asserting my right to honor God's Name in response to its casual use. My stance was clear: if others refrained from using His Name, I would not need to bless His Holy Name in response. (Exodus 20:7)

Mary's spiritual journey, marked by complaints, accusations, misunderstandings, and direct opposition, mirrors the challenges many believers face in living out their faith. While challenging, these experiences indicate a more profound commitment to spiritual growth and are a testament to the strength of steadfast faith.

Standing at the threshold of a new dawn in my faith, I understood that the actual cost of discipleship was not merely a burden to bear but a profound investment in my soul's eternal journey with Christ.

Reflections

Years later, my perspective on Mother Hodge has profoundly shifted. I now recognize her decision to forgive Mr. Hodge's adultery and remain in a marriage devoid of love, not as a weakness but as a tremendous act of strength. She consciously chose to stay, even when she could have left, and ultimately, Mr. Hodge found redemption on his deathbed.

This choice reflects a life deeply rooted in Christ's love and teachings, showing that true fulfillment arises from inner peace and happiness in God, regardless of life's external trials. Mother Hodge's situation is notably rare, as statistics reveal that a mere 5 percent of Christians married to non-believers succeed in converting their spouses. Paying the cost of discipleship is demanding, yet it is also depicted as the pathway to true freedom and victory.

By embracing these costs, believers walk in Christ's authority, overcoming obstacles and challenges that once might have seemed impossible. This transformation process not only reshapes the individual's life but also impacts the world around them through a demonstration of faith, love, and commitment to the principles of the Kingdom of God.

Transformation leads to conformity, and through conformity, it leads to mirroring Christ's image.

How has "paying the cost of discipleship' played out in your life? Share a personal experience where your faith required you to sacrifice or face challenges.

What did you learn about the impact of such sacrifices on your spiritual growth and personal transformation?

CHAPTER 7

Transforming Barriers

Our paths toward spiritual growth are often riddled with barriers that hinder us from fully dedicating ourselves to God. In this chapter, I delve into the personal hurdles I faced, which obstructed my ability to embrace the demands of discipleship wholeheartedly.

The Barrier of Ignorance

My journey commenced with a formidable barrier - ignorance. Initially, I was oblivious to the necessity of my soul's rebirth, and it was my duty to initiate it. This lack of knowledge stunted my spiritual growth. As we've discussed, comprehending spiritual growth entails the crucial role of mind renewal. The state of our mind determines whether we are led by our spiritual essence or driven by our bodily desires.

Transforming the Mind

Paul's powerful call in Romans 12:2 to renew our minds through the transformative power of God's Word was a pivotal moment. This renewal is the rebirth of our soul. Proverbs 4:23 underscores the heart (or soul) as the source of life, urging us to protect it diligently.

This aligns with the understanding of emotions and feelings by emphasizing the importance of being mindful and protective of our inner emotional world, recognizing its profound impact on our actions, decisions, and overall life direction. We must diligently guard it by renewing it with God's Word.

The Dual Nature of "But God"

For me, a significant barrier to embracing the total cost of discipleship was the phrase "But God," which had a dual implication in my spiritual path. Positively, it signified God's timely intervention. However, it also became an excuse for my disobedience and a cause for spiritual stagnation.

Moving Beyond "But God"

Realizing this, I understood that the journey of growth and change commences with a personal decision to transcend the detrimental use of 'But God' and embrace God's will without reservation.

I felt called to start a bible study at home but hesitated, thinking, "But God," I don't know how to teach, and I can't pronounce words accurately." I use "But God" as an excuse to avoid doing God's will.

Embracing God's Will: I decided to take the church challenge and host a small group at our home, overcoming my initial reluctance and aligning my actions with whatever I do; I do it unto the Lord. If I mispronounced a word or talked too much, I did it unto God. Doing it as unto God made the difference for me.

Anger: A Double-Edged Sword

Anger was another significant barrier. It impeded my spiritual growth. There are two forms of anger: righteous and unrighteous. Grasping the distinction, as explained by Dr. Spiros Zodhiates and exemplified by Paul in Ephesians 4:26, was pivotal.

Managing Anger

Our DNA contains an emotion known as anger. The root cause of anger can be either spiritual or physical.

Review Matthew 21:12 and James 4: 1-2 and note your findings. Being angry, I believe, is unavoidable.

It is often associated with sin, but anger isn't always sinful. Paul says, "Be angry and do not sin" (Ephesians 4:26 ESV).

Righteous Versus Unrighteous Anger

In a YouTube message, Dr. Spiros Zodhiates pointed out that anger can be righteous or unrighteous. In Greek, anger has two words. *Orge* is a concept that refers to swallowing up a desire, passion, or emotion and commonly translates as wrath.

This word is in James 1:19, "Wherefore my beloved brethren, let every man be swift to hear, slow to listen, slow to wrath" (KJV).

In other words, wrath is the ability to reach a climax of emotions and passions. The second word is *thumos*, which is anger. Thumos is the outburst of orge or wrath. You are full of feelings and suddenly burst into anger. So, when we talk about being angry, it is both orge, swelling of the emotions, and thumos, the outburst of those emotions.

My temperament was once defined by its quickness to outburst. This underlying spark could rapidly ignite into a fierce blaze, affecting me and those closest to me, particularly when I felt starved of the affection and attention, I believed I deserved. This neglect often led me to think that my anger was justified.

However, Dr. Zodhiates offered a different perspective, emphasizing that genuine, righteous anger should focus on injustices committed against others or the desecration of sacred entities rather than personal grievances. He highlighted the life of Christ as an exemplary, noting how Jesus never reacted in anger to personal slights or offenses against Him. See 1 Peter 2:21.

I learned the importance of letting go and adapting to life's challenges to manage the rising tide of my emotions and prevent them from exploding. This process required a form of self-sacrifice, dying to oneself, to utilize God's power within to overcome my anger. I recognized that it was my responsibility to set aside my wrath.

When faced with irritations, I realized there's always a brief moment before reacting—a critical interval where I can summon the Holy Spirit's strength to temper my swelling emotions before they outburst out of control. This realization is in line with the teachings of Paul in Ephesians 4:26-27 and Colossians 3:8.

Another kryptonite to my putting my anger into submission was softly humming a spiritual hymn—like "Amazing Grace"—.

Prayer, saying "FORGIVEN" to the perpetrator of my pain, taking my gaze off my hurt, and focusing on the verses that speak of anger is akin to a fool; these dissipated my anger (See Psalm 42:5; Colossians 3:1).

The Illusion of Self-Rights

Self-rights are the personal entitlements or demands we feel we deserve based on our views and desires. My supposed self-rights were another hindrance. Because I thought I had self-rights, they kept me from denying myself and carrying my cross because I felt I had autonomy.

Divine Ownership Over Self-Rights

1 Corinthians 6:19-20 (KJV):

What? know ye not that your body is the temple of the Holy Ghost which is in you, which ye have of God, and ye are not your own? For ye are bought with a price: therefore glorify God in your body, and in your spirit, which are God's.

In these powerful verses, Paul communicates profound truths about our identity and purpose as believers. He emphasizes that our bodies are the temple of the Holy Spirit and have been bought at a significant price. Therefore, he urges us to glorify God in our body and spirit. This passage shifts the focus from our rights to our responsibilities towards God.

Recognition of Divine Ownership:

"... ye are not your own?" This portion of the verse strongly challenges the modern, individualistic notion of autonomy. Recognizing that I didn't own myself was pivotal in putting to death my supposed self-rights.

How does the biblical assertion 'ye are not your own' challenge contemporary views on individual autonomy and influence the concept of relinquishing self-claimed rights?

Redeemed at a Price: Unpacking Our Spiritual Purchase:

"For ye are bought with a price ..." reinforces the concept of divine ownership.

What is the" price" mentioned in verse 20, and how does it affect your unequally yoked marriage and life? (See 1 Peter 1:19; Colossians 1:20; Hebrews 9:14)

How does being" bought with a price" challenge your understanding of personal autonomy?

My WHY and Why Me.

In my spiritual growth, I learned that asking God WHY, as exemplified by Job, David, Moses, and even Jesus, is a natural part of the human relationship with Him; it does not contradict faith and obedience. However, these questions can become a barrier to spiritual growth if our "WHY or WHY Me" leads us to harbor and maintain anger toward God.

In a moment of heartfelt vulnerability, I asked God, "Why me? Why do I always have to be the one who humbles myself while CW remains unapologetic?"

This question emerged from a place of deep frustration and hurt. I had been grappling with feelings of injustice and imbalance in my marriage, and CW seemed unaffected by our discord.

As I sat in silence, awaiting an answer, I realized this was more than just a moment of asking why; it was a pivotal point in my spiritual journey. I was standing at the crossroads of bitterness and growth, and the direction I chose would define not just my relationship with CW but also my relationship with God and myself.

In the silence that followed my question, a gentle understanding began to unfold within me. It wasn't about CW's actions or inactions but about my spiritual path and the person I aspired to be. I realized humility wasn't a sign of weakness or submission to unfairness.

Instead, it was a profound strength, a choice to rise above petty conflicts and to embody the grace and love that God extends to me every day. This realization didn't come quickly or easily. It was a struggle against the old me, against the part of me that screamed for justice and recognition.

But in this struggle, I found a deeper connection to God. I understood that my journey wasn't about making CW apologize or change; it was about allowing God to work through me, to mold me into someone who loves unconditionally, who forgives without awaiting an apology, and who finds peace and joy not in the actions of others, but in the closeness of my relationship with God.

My Why became, "Teach me, Lord, to discover the goodness within this painful and hurtful situation."

From Doubt to Conviction: Discovering the Bible's Divine Inspiration

In the first ten years of being saved, I wrestled with a pivotal question: Is the Bible divinely inspired or simply a collection of ancient stories? My curiosity deepened as I considered the authenticity of its stories. Amidst my exploration, I encountered a spectrum of skepticism toward the Bible's veracity.

Voices around me labeled it a tool of oppression, crafted by white men to subjugate others or dismissed as simply outdated. These perspectives left me in a vortex of doubt about the divine origin of the Scriptures.

One night, as I flicked through television channels without purpose, I stumbled upon an old broadcast featuring the esteemed evangelist Billy Graham. As he recounted his past skepticism about the authenticity of the Bible, his words resonated deeply with me.

His dilemma echoed mine: Was the Bible genuinely the word of God or merely a human creation?

Graham faced a pivotal decision in his journey: 'There came a moment when I had to choose — either to trust the limited understanding of humanity or to embrace the boundless wisdom of God.' He decided on God's infinite wisdom.

Alone in the quiet of my room, with Graham's voice, the Holy Spirit conviction struck a chord in me. A moment of revelation washed over me. I took a deep breath and whispered, 'Lord, I believe that through Your divine inspiration, all scripture is given by inspiration of You and is profitable for doctrine, for reproof, for correction, for instruction in righteousness.'

My doubts about the Bible's authenticity were dispelled from that instant. In that quiet moment, a profound peace engulfed me, dispelling my doubts and filling me with unwavering faith. It was a turning point, a realization that faith hinges not on having all the answers but on trusting in the divine wisdom of the Scriptures. With Graham's words as a catalyst, my spiritual journey took a decisive leap forward, ready to embrace the teachings of the Bible with a renewed heart and open mind.

Believing the Bible is God's Word is important because it anchors us in a faith grounded in divine revelation, guides us in living a life that reflects God's love and righteousness, connects us deeply with God and the community of believers, and provides hope and direction throughout life's journey.

Barriers are like threads in the fabric of life, meant to be woven into life with resilience and triumph through Christ.

What spiritual obstacles have you faced, and how did you overcome them? Specifically, how have you dealt with ignorance, reluctance to change, anger, self-righteousness, or doubt? Please share a specific example of how an obstacle has deepened your faith or altered your approach to discipleship.

CHAPTER 8

Spiritual Warfare

The Invisible Battle

In our quiet moments, an unseen conflict rages, transcending the physical realm and touching the very essence of our existence. This is spiritual warfare—a battle within the hearts and minds of every individual, influencing our thoughts, emotions, and actions.

Understanding this hidden war is crucial for living a life of purpose and victory, exploring its origins, impact, and strategies for overcoming adversity.

The concept of spiritual warfare can be understood by tracing its origins. This conflict dates back to a rebellion in the spiritual realm between good and evil, led by the mighty angel Lucifer.

This ongoing struggle continues to impact our world and souls today (see Isaiah 14:12-15, Ezekiel 28:12-17, Revelation 12:7-9).

Spiritual warfare is deeply personal, involving daily battles with sin, demonic influences, and the struggle between good and evil. Believers are called to actively engage in it through prayer, faith, and obedience to God's Word, as it constantly seeks to undermine our faith and divert us from our true purpose—fearing God and obeying His commands.

The story of Eve and the Serpent in the Garden of Eden is one of the earliest and most profound illustrations of spiritual warfare on Earth. This encounter sets the stage for understanding the nature of temptation, deception, and the consequences of our choices.

In the Garden of Eden, the Serpent stole Eve's faith right before her eyes as they were talking face to face, and she didn't even notice. Satan is not a robber but a master thief. The difference between the two is that you know it when you are robbed, but when a thief steals from you, you don't realize it until it's too late.

How did Satan deceive Eve and lead her to disregard God's command?

Now, the Serpent was more cunning than any beast of the field which the Lord God had made. And he said to the woman, "Has God indeed said, 'You shall not eat of every tree of the garden'?" And the woman said to the Serpent, "We may eat the fruit of the trees of the garden; but of the fruit of the tree which is in the midst of the garden, God has said, 'You shall not eat it, nor shall you touch it, lest you die.' Then the Serpent said to the woman, "You will not surely die. For God knows that in the day you eat of it, your eyes will be opened, and you will be like God, knowing good and evil." (Genesis 3:1-5 NKJV)

Deception in Eden

Satan's first tactic in the garden was to instill doubt in Eve's mind by subtly questioning the integrity of God's words. He cleverly used what was true but not truth to deceive her. While it was true that they would not die immediately and would indeed gain knowledge of good and evil, the whole truth was that they would immediately die a spiritual death.

This knowledge would not elevate them but rather make them more like Satan in their disobedience to God. Let's review how Eve allowed these doubts to shift focus from God to self-centered desires.

When Eve saw that the tree was good for food, appealing to the lust of the flesh and pleasant to the eyes, invoking the lust of the eyes, and a tree desirable for gaining wisdom, inciting the pride of life, she ate its fruit. She also gave some to her husband, who was with her, and he ate (Genesis 3:6, John 2:16).

Satan succeeded in his sinister mission. He duped Eve with deception that started in her mind. She was lured by her own desires and tempted. When desire conceives, it gives birth to sin, and sin, when it is fully grown, brings forth spiritual death. Satan stole and undermined their trust in the truthfulness of God's Word, killed their spiritual life by leading them into sin, and destroyed their once-perfect relationship with God. Moreover, when Adam sinned, he inadvertently ceded his God-given authority over the earth to Satan, thus crowning Satan as the prince of this world (Genesis 1:26; Luke 4:6).

The scenes have changed, but Satan's strategies have not. He is still deceiving and setting us up to be drawn away and enticed to sin by our lust of the flesh, the lust of the eyes, and the pride of life to steal, kill, and destroy our faith in God's truth.

The Spiritual Warfare We Face

In John 10:10, Jesus warned that "the thief comes to steal, kill, and destroy. "This thief is Satan. What does he come to steal, kill, and destroy? Our faith and trust in Jesus. He aims to steal our faith and undermine our relationship with God, just as he did with Adam and Eve. On the other hand, Jesus offers abundant life when we walk by faith.

As believers, our faith is our defense against Satan and his destructive ambitions. Luke 18:8 raises the question of whether the Son of Man will find faith on earth upon His return, reminding us of Satan's continuous efforts to diminish our faith amidst prevailing spiritual challenges.

Hebrews 11:6 emphasizes the importance of faith in our relationship with God: "Without faith, it is impossible to please Him. "Faith is crucial and foundational to our spiritual lives. Satan targets our faith because disrupting it can disconnect us from our source of strength.

Paul says, "I have fought the good fight, I have finished the race, I have kept the faith" (2 Timothy 4:7). This verse reminds us that our battle is also about keeping our faith. Satan brings adversity, hoping that we will lose faith in God and each other.

These verses emphasize the intense spiritual warfare surrounding our faith, showcasing its preciousness.

Wrestling with Spiritual Forces

According to Paul in Ephesians 6:12 (KJV), our struggle is not against flesh and blood but against spiritual forces of wickedness. We don't fight these forces; we wrestle with them. Paul's choice of "wrestle" is rooted in the understanding that Jesus' death and resurrection secured victory over sin, death, and Satan. Believers don't fight for victory; we already have it.

Wrestling involves close combat, emphasizing direct contact to immobilize the opponent. Similarly, in spiritual warfare, Satan and his minions aim to immobilize our faith through any means necessary. Losing faith leads to losing hope, love, peace, joy, and purpose. Satan's goal in spiritual warfare is to undermine our faith in God.

Satan begins by targeting our minds, dropping thoughts into them that often manifest through mental and emotional oppression. Through this, Satan sows seeds of doubt, anger, lustful desires, paranoia, revenge, pride, anxiety, loneliness, fear, pain, and confusion to derail us from our faith. He then attempts to destroy us and our relationship with God by enticing us to sin against God's commands through our own lusts.

Spiritual Warfare in an Unequally Yoked Marriage

In an unequally yoked marriage, where one spouse is a believer, and the other is not, Satan finds fertile ground to further his agenda. The differing spiritual perspectives create conflict that arises from opposing spiritual forces, manifesting in differing beliefs that can lure the believing spouse from their faith.

It's a battle that breeds ongoing emotional and spiritual strife and misunderstandings that sever emotional connections, leading to disunity. These issues are not just a passing storm but a constant, looming threat that challenges and strains the marriage and impacts both partners. Satan seeks to exploit the division by fostering misunderstandings, resentment, and spiritual isolation. This leads to frustration, discouragement, and even doubt about the marriage.

In my marriage, spiritual oppression was a constant undercurrent, stemming from our spiritual disconnection and lack of unity. This disunity not only brought tension but became a tool for Satan to plant discord and emotional upheaval.

It turned into a mental and emotional battlefield, heightening my vulnerability to spiritual attacks.

These spiritual attacks were deep spiritual oppression that often felt like an inexplicable heaviness descending upon my heart unexpectedly, even during peaceful times. The spiritual disconnect was a significant source of tension, allowing Satan to sow seeds of discord and emotional turmoil. This daily battle left me vulnerable as if invisible chains weighed down my mind and emotions.

This heaviness wasn't triggered by any specific wrongdoing or fear but seemed to emerge from nowhere, casting a shadow over my well-being. This oppression triggered attitudes toward CW over incidents long past, bewildering him.

Confused and distressed, I cried out to God, seeking answers and clarity. I questioned whether there was any hidden sin in my life or if my faith was lacking. Have I done anything that opened the door for Satan to oppress me?

In seeking clarity, I discovered my spiritual oppression was brought on by my negative thoughts, which had entrenched themselves deeply within my psyche, shaping my perceptions and reactions. Only through the empowering sustenance found in God's promises could I overcome this heavy spiritual oppression.

By focusing on His words and embracing His promises, I found the strength to dispel the oppressive thoughts and regain control over my mind. This journey taught me that while the battle in the mind can be intense, the power of God's Promises provides the ultimate victory over spiritual oppression.

Conquering Spiritual Oppression

God's promises and scripture gave me the strength to conquer this spiritual oppression. Verses like Luke 4:18, John 6:35, Psalms 43:5, and Isaiah 26:3 provided comfort and became my shield and sword.

These scriptures became my shield and sword against the shadows that once defeated me. Standing and feeding off God's strength, His Word, and Jesus's anointing, the Holy Spirit empowered me to dismiss the negative thoughts that invaded my mind. I stopped allowing oppressive thoughts to infiltrate my soul.

It's vital to understand that we constantly face an invisible spiritual battle. Recognizing that these forces take advantage of our weaknesses, such as our thoughts, challenges, desires, and pride, prepares us to be watchful.

I realized the importance of anchoring myself in God's truth and armor: Live by truth, practice righteousness, spread peace, have faith, embrace salvation, and pray for all believers (Ephesians 6:14-18).

When I feel an unexplained heaviness or negative thoughts trying to invade my mind, I remember Paul's advice. I ask myself, "Who is that knocking at my door? Are you true, honest, just, pure, or lovely? Is there anything praiseworthy?" Then, I confidently speak God's promise and stand in Jesus's anointing. I believe that everything God's word says belongs to me in Christ Jesus and is my inheritance.

Spiritual Readiness

Remember to wear God's armor actively and resist the enemy through faith, prayer, love, and obedience to God. Live by truth, practice righteousness, spread peace, have faith, embrace salvation, and stay devoted in prayer for all believers.

Stay persistent, develop spiritual discernment, and counter the enemy's tactics with the truth and power of God's word. By staying connected through prayer and supporting one another in faith, we will conquer Satan's Attacks and live an abundant life, walking in God's grace and peace.

How can believers effectively recognize and counteract Satan's subtle deceptions in spiritual warfare, drawing lessons

from the encounter between Eve and the Serpent in the Garden of Eden?

CHAPTER 9

Distractions

This chapter delves into the intricate web of mindsets that become the heart's traps, intricately weaving our emotions into patterns of negativity towards life or others. It explores how these entwined emotions cultivate a disposition of negativity, which then infiltrates and impacts our relationships, perpetuating a cycle of defeat within us.

In moments when joy seemed distant, I understood that inevitable emotional entanglements were diminishing the Lord's joy in my life. This journey to clarity began with an insightful revelation from the Holy Spirit, who used the scripture of Luke 10:40 to illuminate the root causes of this fading joy.

"But Martha was cumbered about much serving, and came to him, and said, Lord, dost thou not care that my sister hath left me to serve alone? Bid her therefore that she help me." (KJV)

This passage mirrored my distractions and anxieties, overshadowing my ability to find joy in Christ. This scriptural insight was a turning point, guiding me to realize that joy in the Lord is not determined by our external situations but by where we place our attention and hearts.

Upon studying this verse, I identified four distinct snares of the heart exemplified in Martha's life. Martha's story illustrates how negative emotions can trap us, obstructing the joy of Christ in our lives. I aim to dissect these distractions, offering insights into their nature and how I navigated through them to reclaim and retain the joy of the Lord in my heart.

Distraction 1: Complaining (Luke 10:40):

My journey through the maze of marital dissatisfaction began with a habitual tendency to complain, much like Martha in the biblical account of Luke 10:40, who expressed her frustration to Jesus about Mary not helping her. Similarly, I found myself frequently voicing complaints about my husband. My prayers often echoed this discontent, focusing on his perceived lack of appreciation and support.

This constant stream of complaints and finding fault wasn't just a personal habit; it created a noticeable rift in my family. It strained my relationship with CW and cast a shadow over our household, affecting our children. Acknowledging the need for change, I delved into the roots of my dissatisfaction. Discovering that these complaints were the surface expressions of more profound, unresolved feelings of unforgiveness, bitterness, and resentment was a revelation.

To break this cycle, I involved my children in a unique strategy: a game where they would earn a token reward every time they heard me comment negatively about their father. This approach was enlightening. It made me realize how my offhand remarks, which I considered harmless, were interpreted as complaints by my children. For instance, my comments about CW leaving groceries unpacked, which I considered casual observations, were seen as complaining.

Seeking a shift in perspective, I started to view and refer to CW in a more positive light as the 'king of our home.' I tried to instill a sense of celebration around his daily return from work, encouraging our children to welcome him enthusiastically. However, I noticed that old habits die hard; I sometimes slipped back into complaining, especially if CW's reaction did not match our excitement.

This was a crucial realization, helping me see these instances as pitfalls leading back to negativity. I hadn't considered that perhaps the man, weary from a long day's work, wished for some rest.

The game with the children was more than just a playful exercise; it was a profound lesson in self-awareness. It illuminated the fact that my habit of complaining and finding fault was not just a nuisance but a gateway to deeper emotional issues and spiritual stagnation, as highlighted in Philippians 2:14.

Inspired by the scripture in Colossians 3:23, which advocates doing everything wholeheartedly as if for the Lord. When I tried adopting a mindset to serve CW as if serving Christ was a challenge, despite my best efforts, I often found myself murmuring and complaining when CW's responses didn't meet my expectations. However, with the Holy Spirit's guidance, I began to evaluate whether my actions were for Christ or my self-interest. Acts did for Christ brought peace, regardless of CW's reactions, because they were offered to Jesus.

In contrast, any act of kindness that left me angry or resentful was a clear sign that it was motivated by self-gratification rather than a genuine desire to serve CW as done unto Christ.

This understanding became a pivotal tool in overcoming my inclination to complain and find fault, leading me toward emotional and spiritual growth.

Distraction 2: Doubting Divine Care

Amid life's turmoil, I echo Martha's poignant query to Jesus in Luke 10:40, "Lord, don't you care?"

This question arose from my depths during personal crises, such as health problems, the loss of a job, or struggles within my marriage. It was a heartfelt cry, questioning the presence and love of God in my life's most challenging chapters.

This mindset was a distraction, steering me away from trusting in God's love and plan for me. As Paul describes in the epistles, it was a fight to keep faith against spiritual forces that sought to immobilize it. This struggle was not a physical battle but a spiritual wrestling, requiring steadfast faith in God's supremacy and grace.

I have learned that during times of doubt, I must remain faithful and sustain myself by standing and feeding off God's strength by speaking His Word, allowing its truth to resonate and impact my situation.

Distraction 3: Loneliness and Its Deceptions

Loneliness was another significant snare, mirroring Martha's feeling of abandonment in her tasks," my sister left me to serve alone. Martha was alone, but I was lonely. This loneliness was not just about physical isolation but an emotional void, a longing for deeper connection and understanding with CW.

The Ignored Pleas for Connection

My attempts to connect with my spouse should have been noticed. This disregard for my feelings deepened my isolation, like an unwatered flower wilting without care. Loneliness is difficult in a marriage. It can also open doors to temptation, as I experienced. Craving admiration and affection from my husband, I was drawn to another man who seemed to fulfill these emotional voids.

A new colleague at work became a source of this attraction. Initially, there was no allure, but over time, through shared conversations and laughter, I felt a forbidden desire grow. Despite knowing it was wrong, I fantasized about him, realizing I had committed mental adultery.

A Moment of Realization and Repentance

During a Bible study on James 1:13−16, I had a profound realization. I understood that my attraction was not a result of external forces but instead, it was rooted in my lustful desires. This understanding led me to follow the scriptural guidance, to confess and seek forgiveness for these thoughts. The relief and liberation I felt after this confession was genuinely transformative.

After my confession, I experienced a profound change; my attraction to my colleague vanished. When he persisted in his advances, I discovered a newfound strength within me and firmly rejected him. No longer a volunteer to his sweet nothings, my resolve revealed his true nature. He called me derogatory names and admitted he never liked me. His subsequent criminal activities confirmed the danger I had narrowly escaped. I saw him on television for robbery. God knew I wanted to be kept, and He kept me. Thank you, Jesus.

Through this experience, I've learned to combat loneliness by finding solace in the glorification of God through worship and prayer. Listening to worship music, I discovered comfort and strength in repeating the lyrics, which reminded me of God's omnipresence, boundless love, and holiness, unwaveringly trusting His promises; even when His immediate presence wasn't felt, I prayed His Word back to Him and ultimately found profound peace.

Distraction 4: Commanding God

Continuing my introspection into Luke 10:40, I identified the distraction of demanding action from God, similar to Martha's command to Jesus to bid Mary to come and help her. I also commanded God to change CW's ways. Martha sought Jesus' intervention regarding Mary's choice to sit at His feet, and Jesus' response was unexpected.

He defended Mary's decision, emphasizing the importance of focusing on spiritual nourishment and learning from Him, which is crucial. He says, "Martha, Martha, thou art careful and troubled about many things: But one thing is needful: and Mary hath chosen that good part, which shall not be taken away from her."

This response highlights the importance of choosing what is essential – the 'good part' Mary chose: devoting herself to Christ, His teachings, and her part in the Kingdom of God, a choice that brings lasting fulfillment and cannot be taken away.

In Jesus' response to Martha, I found a reflection of His message. It highlighted that I had lost focus on the most essential thing – prioritizing God's Kingdom. This insight illuminated the fact that I was the one in need of change, not CW. It also explained why the joy of the LORD had wandered in my life.

Embracing Spiritual Focus: A Path to Deeper Connection with God

If you recognize yourself in these scenarios – getting caught up in complaints, feeling doubts about God's involvement in your life, experiencing a sense of emotional isolation, or trying to control divine outcomes – understand that these are snares of being distracted from prioritizing God's Kingdom.

These distractions act as joy killers, diminishing your enthusiasm once held. It's a signal that your focus has shifted to the wrong things. To navigate these challenges, it is essential to get back on track by refocusing on your relationship with God.

This involves seeking His guidance in every challenge, taking your mind off yourself, letting go of the negative feelings, delving deeper into His word and applying it to your life, even when it hurts, trusting His plan, and doing whatever you do for others as doing it unto Christ. Such steps bring you back onto the spiritual track and deepen your connection with God, leading you back to the joy of the Lord.

Distraction's whispers deceive, like a siren's song, leading hearts astray.

CHAPTER 10

The Evolution of Love and Faith

Navigating an unequally yoked marriage presents unique challenges and opportunities for spiritual growth.

The journey through stages of faith—from dormant to little and finally to great faith—parallels the deepening of affection for God, moving from liking to loving and ultimately falling in love with God with all my heart, soul, mind, and strength was pivotal in overcoming the complexities and hardships inherent in such a relationship.

Here's how each stage of faith and affection impacted my unequally yoked marriage.

Dormant Faith and Liking God:

The dormant faith stage of my spiritual walk can be best described as a dimly lit candle in a vast room of uncertainty and trials. My faith was constantly challenged by doubt and fear, like a candle flickering in the wind. Liken to the disciples in Mark 4:40-41, afraid despite Jesus's presence during a storm.

Jesus spoke to His disciples: "Why are you so afraid? Do you still have no faith?" These words mirror my experience; my faith was inactive, akin to Jesus's slumbering in the boat, needing to be roused and strengthened by renewed confidence in His guidance and care.

I acknowledged His existence and appreciated my salvation. The dormancy of my faith at this stage significantly limited my following Christ's teachings only when it was convenient, mirroring my 'liking affection' for Him. For instance, I would pray and seek God's guidance in times of need but be unwilling to obey if it cost me. Challenges quickly shook my faith, and my affection for Christ was more about seeking comfort than genuinely desiring to live in His likeness.

This passive faith and casual affection for God meant that arguments and my emotional outbursts often characterized my response to the spiritual discord in my marriage with a weak spiritual foundation and liking for God and navigating the differences in belief and practice within my marriage, which led to my walking in the flesh, which led to tension and misunderstanding.

At that point in my journey, I had yet to obey Christ fully, mainly because I had yet to fully embrace the demands of discipleship, which are necessary to wield Christ's authority effectively.

Little Faith and Loving God:

Navigating through a pivotal period of personal crisis, my faith in God, initially as fragile as the disciples amidst a storm, began to solidify. This transformation mirrored Peter's attempt to walk on water towards Jesus (Matthew 14:29-31), where his faltering steps underlined my doubts. Yet, in choosing to trust Jesus amidst my fears, my faith and love for Him deepened significantly.

This shift became apparent in how I responded to personal conflicts, particularly with my husband. Rather than react from a place of hurt, I turned to prayer, guided not by ease but by a commitment to follow Christ's teachings on forgiveness. This act of faith, challenging as it was, exemplified the profound impact of God's love and patience on my spiritual journey, teaching me that true devotion emerges from trusting God through life's storms.

This deeper emotional and spiritual connection with Jesus influenced my perspective and actions within my marriage. I was more proactive in demonstrating God's love to my spouse. Despite the growth of my faith and my deepening love for God, I found that my obedience was not without its conditions, hindered by a tangle of doubts and fears.

A fierce clinging to my perceived rights, an unhealthy dependence on CW, and my battle with low self-esteem all formed a barrier between me and complete surrender to God.

More than anything, it was my fear of appearing weak that held me back, coupled with the terror of losing what I thought I couldn't live without. This complex web of fears and dependencies prevented me from offering my whole self to God, as the thought of losing control over my life, represented by my concern over losing CW, loomed large in my heart.

Great Faith and Falling in Love with God:

My journey to 'great faith' and a deep love for God was fueled by His unwavering faithfulness, love, and grace. This divine grace revealed His kindness and blessings, inspiring me to reciprocate with trust and love. This connection to God's grace reshaped how I viewed my challenging marriage, encouraging me to approach it with grace and understanding instead of frustration.

This transformation led me to a profound commitment: to love CW unconditionally despite the lack of reciprocation and the demands it placed on me. My motivation to persevere through these trials was rooted in a sincere love for Christ and a firm belief in His purpose for my life.

My faith and love were tested as I grappled with feelings of emotional abandonment and not being a priority in CW's life. When I confronted him, expressing my feelings of being sidelined and discussing the importance of me in his life went on deaf ears. During these times, God taught me self-love and loving CW through challenging times, even when I felt overlooked.

The resolution of this test deepened my dependence on Christ for my needs. It also reminded me that striving to love as God does requires sacrifice, continuous effort, understanding, and willingness to put God's commands above one's own for spiritual growth's sake.

The Essence of Sacrificial Love

Abraham's faith and love toward God epitomized the ultimate act of obedience - the willingness to sacrifice his only son, Isaac, as an act of service to God. In relinquishing his self-rights and freedom of choice out of love for God, Abraham demonstrated the true power of sacrificial faith and love.

Similarly, when we love God with all our heart, soul, mind, strength, and might, we align ourselves with His will, bringing all His commands and decrees into harmony with our lives, knowing if we sacrifice what we hold dear to our hearts for His sakes as illustrated by Abraham, we demonstrate our ultimate trust and faith in His plan, experiencing the profound depth of His love and the transformative power of genuine devotion.

A servant of God

In James 1, James refers to himself as a 'servant' of God and the Lord Jesus Christ. Here, the Greek term 'doulos' conveys a deeper meaning than just a servant. It signifies someone who has relinquished personal freedom, becoming wholly an instrument in their master's hands, unable to refuse any command.

When slavery still existed in parts of the South, a young man was being auctioned, and an Englishman eventually won the bid.

When the young man derisively pointed out that slavery was abolished in England, the Englishman revealed he bought him to set him free. Overwhelmed, the young man vowed to serve him willingly for life.

The story of the Englishman liberating a young man from slavery eloquently symbolizes our spiritual servitude to God, illustrating profound truths about redemption and voluntary service.

The Englishman, motivated by compassion rather than obligation, frees the young man, who, in turn, chooses to serve him out of gratitude, not necessity.

This mirrors our relationship with God, who liberates us from sin's bondage through Jesus's sacrifice—akin to the Englishman's purchase—not because of our worthiness but due to His immense love, grace, and mercy.

Recognizing the profoundness of my spiritual freedom inspired me to serve God willingly, driven by love and gratitude rather than obligation, embracing my role as a joyful servant in response to the ultimate gift of liberation He provides. The progression from initial uncertainty to complete surrender highlights the essence of spiritual growth and my behavior toward my unbeliever.

This path leads me to embrace Christ's characteristics in guiding my actions and decisions toward my husband. Navigating this journey, I've come to trust in God's guidance, relinquishing my desires in His favor. The process was excruciating, resembling the death of my ego, as I endeavored to emulate God's love toward others.

This surrender, far from a passive submission, represents a deliberate effort to harmonize my wishes with God's intentions. It paves the way to a life embodying faith manifested in love, service, obedience, and sacrifice. While loving God involves respect and reverence, being in love with God encompasses a far more profound devotion marked by sacrifice.

In my journey through varying levels of faith and affection for God within my unequally yoked marriage, I have discovered profound lessons about myself, God's grace, and the role of faith and love in fostering patience and understanding.

I invite you to embark on a path of personal reflection and proactive steps toward growth. Here's how you might begin this transformative journey:

1. **Reflect on Your Spiritual Path:** Take some quiet time to contemplate your current stage of faith and feelings towards God. Are you in a dormant or little faith phase, or have you reached a place of great faith? How does your affection for God—liking, loving, or profoundly falling in love—affect your obedience towards God at each stage?

2. **Identify Areas for Spiritual Growth:** With honest introspection, pinpoint areas in your spiritual life and marriage where you aspire to grow. Consider setting specific, achievable goals to deepen your connection with God and enhance your spiritual journey.

3. **Communicate Openly with Your Spouse:** Engage in heartfelt discussions about your faith journey with your spouse, emphasizing empathy and understanding.

4. **Commit to Prayer:** Tell God your problems before talking to others about them. Dedicate time to pray for guidance, wisdom, and the fortitude to face the complexities of an unequally yoked marriage with grace. Pray, too, for your spouse that their heart may be touched by God's love in unexpected ways.

5. **Embrace Unconditional Love:** Let unconditional love be your guiding principle in your interactions and responses within your marriage. Unconditional love does not imply enduring harmful, disrespectful, or degrading behavior; it has boundaries. Let God's unconditional love for you be your guide. This type of love requires wisdom, discernment, and knowing when to step back. Remember, takers have no bounds; thus, you must set the limits.

6. **Trust God's Plan:** Remember the importance of trusting God's overarching plan. This trust can bring peace amid uncertainty and strength to overcome challenges.

7. **Seek Support from a Faith Community:** After grounding yourself in divine consultation through prayer, you may find solace and support in a community or among individuals who can provide meaningful advice, encouragement, and a sense of belonging as you tackle your unique challenges.

By taking these steps, you open yourself to a profound personal and spiritual development journey. Each step is an opportunity to deepen your faith, strengthen your marriage, and live a rich life aligned with God's love and purpose.

Your level of faith and love for God distinguishes obedience from disobedience.

Reflecting on your transformative journey of faith amidst personal and marital challenges, how does moving from doubt to deep trust in God mirror the biblical accounts of Peter's walk on water and Abraham's willingness to sacrifice Isaac?

How do these scriptural examples inspire your actions and mindset in dealing with conflicts and fears, especially within an unequally yoked marriage?

CHAPTER 11

My Identity in Christ

The Heartbreak at the Barbershop

Imagine the profound pain of hearing your life partner say publicly, "I love my wife, but I'm not in love with her." This shocking revelation came from CW at his brother's barbershop. The love of my life, whom I'd devoted sixteen years to, had casually stripped away the essence of my hope. Imagine the profound pain of hearing your life partner say publicly, "I love my wife, but I'm not in love with her." This shocking revelation came from CW at his brother's barbershop.

How could he expose such intimate feelings without a prior conversation with me? The moment he uttered those heart-shattering words at his brother's barbershop, it was more than just a public humiliation; it was an affirmation of the painful truth I had silently harbored—his lack of love for me. As I sat silently in the car as we drove home, tears cascaded down my cheeks. The agony of this public revelation was overwhelming, a stark contrast to the silent suffering of our private lives.

Back home, my bottled-up emotions erupted. "You love me, but you're not in love with me?" I demanded, confronting his emotionless gaze. His silence was deafening, more hurtful than any words. When I pressed him further, seeking the reason for his love, his response was cruel: he loved me only as the mother of his children. At that moment, I realized his love for me was no different from his feelings for the mothers of his other children. Consumed by sorrow, I found the courage to voice the question that haunted me: "Why do you stay if you are not in love with me?" His response, tinged with uncertainty and resignation, was a simple, "I don't know."

The weight of his words hung heavily in the air, reflecting a perplexing mix of emotions and unanswered questions. Life has a unique way of catching our attention, often through unexpected means. My life revolved around CW, making him the pivot of my happiness. His words fell like heavy stones, publicly exposing the fragility of our relationship and leaving me raw and vulnerable.

His approval was the barometer of my self-worth. A casual remark about my makeup, "he could tell when my makeup was wearing off," shattered my confidence. While our intimacy was confined to the bedroom, his public denial was the awakening I needed.

A Harsh Awakening

This admission illuminated the hidden corners of our marriage. It explained CW's persistent indifference, unjustified anger, and reluctance to include me in his social circle. I remembered my hurt words, "You don't take me anywhere except with our family. No one else knows I'm your wife."

I also saw the truth behind our intimate moments. CW's passionate lovemaking, which I had clung to as a sign of hope, was now revealed as a mere act devoid of genuine affection. It was a devastating realization that a man could be passionately physically intimate without being in love with you. This profound realization hit me like a ton of bricks, making me understand that I had been clinging to a version of our relationship that may have never truly existed. CW's words were a catalyst, igniting a self-pity party within me. My guests included despair, anxiety, and a deep sense of low self-esteem. This self-esteem issue brought along loneliness, frustration, and regret. Regret, in turn, invited bitterness, resentment, and anger.

Anger declared that no real party was complete without tears, prompting them to join. I lay there, feeling victimized, not realizing that after the initial shock, I became a volunteer, willingly subjecting myself to emotional turmoil. I began to understand that my wallowing in despair, anxiety, and bitterness was not just a response to external circumstances but also a result of my unwillingness to face the truths in my life and marriage.

The depth of my self-loathing intensified as I reflected on our marriage's inception. It dawned on me that I had coerced CW into marriage by my ultimatum that he agreed to because it was more about convenience for him than genuine affection for me.

A Spiritual Epiphany

As I lay in bed amidst the swirling storm of my thoughts, the phrase "For I am not ashamed of the Gospel of Christ, for it is the power of God" surfaced in my thoughts. This line echoed in my mind, not once but thrice. Intrigued and curious, I rose from the bed and fetched my Bible. Upon locating the verse in Romans 1:16, I was perplexed as to why that verse popped into my thoughts. A cross-reference to 1 Corinthians 15:3-4 delved into the profound subjects of Christ's death, burial, and resurrection.

I was initially baffled by the unexpected intrusion of Romans 1:16 into my thoughts, especially since I was versed in the gospel's essence – Christ's death, burial, and resurrection. In my quest for understanding, I sought clarity from God on why this particular verse had surfaced in my mind. During this moment of inquiry, the Holy Spirit intervened, guiding me to a deeper examination. I was led to delve into each event of Jesus's death, burial, and resurrection and consider the significance of His ascension.

This directed introspection opened up a more nuanced and comprehensive appreciation of the power of the gospel's depth and breadth in my life.

- **Jesus's Death:** This symbolizes deliverance from the grip of sin, death, God's wrath, Satan, and sinful tendencies like pride, lying, evil desire, fornication, and emotional turmoil like self-pity, victim mentality, resentment, etc. I came to understand that I was

shackled by things from which Jesus's death had already set me free. (Romans 6:17-18)
- **Jesus's Burial**: This symbolizes death to my old dominion nature, empowering me to overcome my inherent sinful tendencies, a transformation facilitated by my baptism into Jesus's burial. Jesus's burial gave me the power to overcome what once conquered me: my flesh's dominion, sin, and emotional turmoil. (Romans 6:4a)
- **Christ's Resurrection**: This signifies a new quality of life, a newness of life. The new life in Christ involves a new spiritual nature, abundant life, spiritual blessings, and using Christ's authority over sin, Satan, and emotional oppression while embodying Christ's righteousness, teachings, and values, such as love, compassion, and humility, in daily living to honor God and prepare for eternal life. (Romans 6:4b)
- **Christ's Ascension** - Symbolizes the fulfillment of God's numerous promises, the foremost being the gift of Divine Assistance, the Holy Spirit. While these promises are plentiful, we must fulfill God's conditions to reap their benefits. (John 16:7)

In a moment of emotional release, I was overwhelmed with tears as a profound realization washed over me. I had been living in self-imposed captivity, oblivious to the power and freedom that Christ's sacrificial love had granted me through His death, burial, and resurrection.

I had languished in imagined bondage, not recognizing that I had been set free, and this moment of clarity marked a significant shift in my life, prompting me to step into my true identity, liberty, and wholeness that Christ had always intended for me. Perhaps you have heard of the story of the little bird. The bird had his wing over his eye, and he was crying. The owl said to the little bird you are crying. Yes, said the little bird as he pulled his wing from his eye.

"Oh, I see," said the owl. "You're crying because the big bird pecked out your eye." The little bird said, "No, I am not crying because the big bird pecked out my eye. I am crying because I let Him."

For years, I had been like that little bird, allowing my circumstances and the actions of others to dictate my feelings and responses, not realizing the power of the gospel of Christ's death, burial, and resurrection had liberated me.

It dawned on me that the power to change my story through the power of the gospel of Christ was always in my hands; I had ignorantly allowed it to slip through my fingers like grains of sand. I had spent so much time with my wing over my eye, blinded by my tears and engulfed by self-pity, that I failed to see my identity in Christ. I was a beloved child of God with divine lineage and purpose. I was bestowed with spiritual blessings in Christ, yet I lived as a peasant when I was of royal heritage.

Like the bird, I wasn't crying because of what was done to me but because I had permitted it to define me, to shape the contours of my life in ways that left me feeling powerless and small. This revelation of Christ's death, burial, and resurrection, plus promises, signaled the start of a new quality of life, and understanding of my identity in Christ came with a profound sense of empowerment.

I understood that while I couldn't change the past, I could influence my future. I was given the authority to take my pen back and write my story. I could decide not to let the actions of others define me. So, I began to lift my wing from my eye, to wipe away the tears, and to see the world anew.

Like the little bird, I recognized that my true power lay not in avoiding pain or adversity but in choosing to utilize the power in the gospel of Christ. This story of the little bird and the wise owl became more than a tale of sorrow; it transformed into a narrative of awakening, of coming into one's power through Christ's expository death, burial, and resurrection, and recognizing that the people who know their God will be strong and do great exploits.

How could embracing your identity in Christ—rooted in His death, burial, and resurrection as depicted in Scripture—transform the conclusion of your life's story?

CHAPTER 12

The Sacred Wilderness

In God's design, the wilderness is not a place of despair but a sacred nurturing incubator where personal growth and profound revelations occur. It is a place where difficulties offer unparalleled insight into God Himself, promising a transformative journey for those who embrace it.

Consider the story of Hagar, the Egyptian servant of Sarai and Abram, later known as Sarah and Abraham. Hagar's journey into the wilderness was born from personal strife. Sarai, unable to have children, gave Hagar to Abram, hoping to fulfill God's promise of a great lineage.

However, Hagar's subsequent pregnancy led to a bitter fallout with Sarai, driving her into the wilderness. In this desolation, she encountered an angel of the Lord. She had a profound epiphany, recognizing God as 'El Roi,' the God who sees her plight (See Genesis 16:9).

In her solitary journey through the wilderness, Hagar, a woman of remarkable resilience, reached a transformative juncture. This desolate setting became the backdrop for a profound revelation: God's awareness of her anguish and His willingness to intervene at crucial junctures. God acknowledged her distress and instructed her to return and yield to Sarai, emphasizing the virtues of humility and obedience, even under trying circumstances.

Throughout these times, Hagar learned that she was not invisible; God was present, observant, and affirming of her in her most challenging moments. Like Hagar, I, too, found myself in a similar situation, fleeing my unequally yoked marriage with my children and seeking solace at my mother's home.

A divine nudge compelled me to return to my husband, a decision that felt like stepping back into a world of pain, especially when met with disdain. Yet, in this journey of return and subsequent retreats in the wilderness, particularly our local park, God's comforting words echoed:

"So do not fear, for I am with you; do not be dismayed, for I am your God. I will strengthen you and help you; I will uphold you with my righteous right hand." (Isaiah 41:10 NIV).

Months went by, and the dynamics of my marriage remained unchanged. Seeking solace in the wilderness of the local park, a cascade of scriptures illuminated my shortcomings as a wife:

"Wives, be subject to your husbands," "Wives, respect your husbands," "Wives, let your actions speak, adorned in the virtues of gentleness and meekness, much like the holy women of the past who put their trust in God."

(Ephesians 5:22, 33; 1 Peter 3:1–6 paraphrased).

These scriptures became my guide, inspiring me to grow and learn from my failed tests. Gentleness and meekness are powerful virtues. Gentleness is the grace to remain kind despite adversity, while meekness is the strength to relinquish control, trusting that God is the ultimate helmsman.

I wondered how to embrace a submissive role when my husband, with his laid-back nature, didn't appear eager to take the lead in our household. However, as I learned to be cloaked in these virtues, I began to perceive the trials through a lens softened by divine grace. In the crucible of this wisdom, gentleness emerged as a benevolent guide, encouraging a compassionate response amid adversity.

In the wilderness, navigating the complexities of an unequally yoked marriage, I found an unexpected kinship with the apostle Paul and his struggle with a 'thorn in the flesh. This challenging terrain became the backdrop for a pivotal realization: my feelings of inadequacy, the yearning for love and self-worth, and CW's emotional detachment were not stumbling blocks but avenues for experiencing God's grace.

This change in outlook was not immediate or accessible. It necessitated letting go of my preconceived ideas and an earnest effort to recognize God in every aspect of my marriage. I began to perceive these struggles as not obstacles but divine assignments to test and strengthen my faith and love.

This approach transformed my spirit into a fertile ground for spiritual growth. Each challenge pushed me closer to understanding God's aim to refine me and instill in me qualities such as empathy, patience, and forgiveness—hallmarks of Christ's character.

Six Pillars of Spiritual Transformation

Embarking on a divine-led journey through the wilderness, I discovered six essential pillars that became powerful tools in conquering the consequences inherited in an unequally yoked marriage: faith, prayer, mind renewal, loving God wholly, dying to myself, and loving myself with God's divine love.

These pillars simultaneously empowered me to walk in my spiritual blessings in heavenly places and utilize Christ's authority, enabling me to live out my commitment to Him profoundly and tangibly, facing challenges with strength and resilience.

Faith

Faith is the bedrock of one's relationship with God, beginning with a divinely inspired desire to know and trust Him. It empowers individuals to believe in the unseen and follow Jesus, even when the path is unclear. Without faith, one cannot please God, but with it, one demonstrates one's trust in His will.

Faith is not merely a belief; it is a call to action. By obeying God's commandments, individuals show their trust in His will.

Romans 10:17 teaches that faith grows through engaging with the Word of Christ and hearing testimonies, while challenges deepen one's trust, as highlighted in James 1:2-4.

According to Hebrews 11:1, faith is the assurance of things hoped for and the conviction of things not seen, anchoring individuals in spiritual realities beyond visible circumstances.

James 2:17 emphasizes that true faith compels action, not just belief, urging individuals to live out God's commandments and demonstrate their trust through deeds.

Jesus' metaphor in Matthew 17:20, about faith as small as a mustard seed, shows that its effectiveness isn't limited by size but by sincerity.

Finally, 2 Corinthians 5:7 calls individuals to walk by faith, focusing on spiritual truths rather than observable conditions, which will guide them through life's uncertainties and bring them closer to God.

Trusting God, regular study, reflection, and seeking understanding are practical ways I strengthen my faith, helping me resolve doubts and believe more profoundly.

Prayer

Prayer is an intimate conversation with God, essential for profoundly connecting with His presence; it allows individuals to seek guidance, express gratitude, and find comfort.

Philippians 4:6 teaches us to approach God with all our concerns and thankfulness.

James 5:16 encourages powerful and effective transparent, confessional prayer, while Matthew 6:6 highlights the importance of private, sincere conversations with God in solitude.

1 Thessalonians 5:17 urges us to pray persistently and maintain a continuous dialogue with God throughout the day, and Psalm 145:18 reassures us that God is near whenever we call on Him truthfully.

These scriptures underscore the transformative power of prayer in our lives, guiding and enriching our spiritual journey.

To cultivate a vibrant prayer life:

1. Set aside specific times each day for prayer.
2. Dedicate a peaceful spot free from distractions.
3. Use Scripture as a guide.
4. Keep a Prayer Journal for reflections and insights.
5. Embrace the silence, allowing space for God to speak.
6. Engage in communal prayer for encouragement and support.

Developing a vibrant prayer life takes time and commitment. Persist through challenging times, trusting that God is always near and listening.

Mind Renewal

Our journey of renewing the mind has been profoundly transformative, greatly influenced by the guiding light of Scripture.

Romans 12:2 teaches us to resist the world's patterns and instead allow our minds to be renewed, leading to an understanding of God's good, pleasing, and perfect will.

Ephesians 4:23 inspires us to adopt a fresh mental and spiritual attitude, while Colossians 3:2 focuses on divine truths away from earthly distractions.

Philippians 4:8 further encouraged us to contemplate true, noble, proper, pure, lovely, and admirable things, nurturing positive and informative thoughts.

Our active pursuit of this renewal involves daily Bible reading and prayer for the Holy Spirit's guidance, which has deepened our understanding and application of God's Word.

We find solace in meditating on Scripture, memorizing key verses, and striving to apply Biblical principles in daily life. The invaluable support and enriched understanding gained from being part of a Bible study group have significantly contributed to our spiritual growth.

Obedience to God's Word is not just a choice but a clear indicator of our mind's renewal. We regularly assess our lives against Scripture, remaining open to the Holy Spirit's conviction and striving to lead lives that glorify God.

This commitment to obedience is a testament to the transformation happening within us, a sign of our renewed mind.

Loving God with All Your Being

Loving God with all one's being is the core of spiritual devotion. It prioritizes Him above all else and aligns thoughts, actions, and emotions with His will. This command requires sacrifices, enduring trials, and giving up comforts for a deeper relationship with God. Our commitment to loving God with all our soul, spirit, mind, and strength is driven by gratefulness and a heartfelt desire to know and please Him.

Guided by Mark 12:30 and Deuteronomy 6:5, we are learning to love God wholly and unreservedly. We cultivate this love by praying, worshiping, and studying Scripture, as Psalm 63:1 expresses our soul's thirst for God in a dry and weary land.

John 14:15-17 deepens this commitment as Jesus promises the Holy Spirit to help us love Him and keep His commandments, enhancing our understanding of God's love and guiding our spirit.

1 Corinthians 6:20 reminds us that our body is a temple of the Holy Spirit, urging us to honor God with our physical being.

These scriptures inspire us to integrate our love for God in every action, thought, and moment, striving to reflect His love and glory in all we do.

This love continues transforming us, aligning our desires with His, and fuels our ability to face challenges with faith and courage.

Dying to Yourself

Dying to oneself is an active and transformative journey deeply rooted in our walk with God, fueled by a profound love for Jesus. It is a journey that revolves around Scriptures such as Galatians 2:20, which boldly declares, 'I have been crucified with Christ, and I no longer live, but Christ lives in me.'

This verse encapsulates our commitment to surrendering personal desires and living under Christ's guidance.

1 Corinthians 6:19-20 reminds us that we do not belong to ourselves, having been bought at a price, Jesus's blood, which urges us to honor God with our body and spirit.

Philippians 3:10 expresses our active yearning to know Christ and the power of His resurrection, to share in His sufferings, and to become like Him in His death.

This active walk of self-denial brings us closer to the essence of Christ's life and sacrifice. Through these teachings, we actively strive to continually lay down our lives, allowing Christ's life to be magnified in us, which actively transforms our understanding and experience of actual life in Him. To die to ourselves, we acknowledged our need for change and an understanding of God's unconditional love and grace. It involved:

- Surrendering our desires and ambitions.
- Putting others' needs before our own.
- Serving without expectation of return.
- Whatever we do, we do it as unto Jesus.

This journey requires grace, humility, patience, and a significant reshaping of priorities to reflect Christ's teachings. It is a continuous process of surrendering to God's will, leading to a deeper connection with Him and a more fulfilling life in His service.

Loving Myself as God Loves Me

Embracing self-love, deeply rooted in the divine love with which God cherishes us, is beneficial and essential for our spiritual and emotional well-being.

Scriptures like Jeremiah 31:3, Ephesians 2:4-5, and 1 John 4:16 serve as powerful reminders of God's unconditional and everlasting love, urging us to embrace ourselves with the same compassion and acceptance that God shows us but also allows His divine love to reflect in how we treat ourselves and interact with others. Our journey to love ourselves with divine love, as God loves us, commences with a deep understanding of God's unconditional love. We affirm our worth based on His love, not external appearances or achievements. We practice gratitude, set healthy boundaries, and care for our physical, emotional, and spiritual well-being by standing on the firm foundation of affirmations rooted in Scripture.

This process liberates us from self-doubt and insecurity, empowering us to embrace our unique beauty and worth. Emerging from the 'wilderness,' I realized that God's design was never about the wilderness itself but what it represented in my spiritual walk: a place of testing, growth, conformity, and deep communion with God.

These six pillars—faith, prayer, mind renewal, loving God wholly, dying to oneself, and loving oneself as God loves us—guided me through difficult times and helped me conquer challenges in my life.

It wasn't easy to walk to grow spiritually, but the rewards and the sense of fulfillment were beyond measure, inspiring me to continue on this path.

How does Chapter 10 depict the wilderness as a catalyst for personal transformation and a deeper understanding of purpose?

CHAPTER 13

Tribulation for a Purpose

The dining table was set, but there was a noticeable absence. CW, once again, chose to isolate himself from our family dinner. His persistent avoidance of these shared moments left a void that was hard to ignore. As I glanced towards him, I couldn't help but yearn for his presence.

However, he was engrossed in the television news, seemingly oblivious to our family's dynamics. His attention was elsewhere, and it was a painful realization. This was a recurring scene in our household, one that I had grown accustomed to over the years.

A mix of frustration and resentment simmered within me. Unable to contain it any longer, I let out a sarcastic remark, "Why can't you join us for dinner? Or perhaps the news holds more important than your own family?" I added bitterly, "Oh, I almost forgot — a family wasn't what you wanted in the first place!"

CW glanced in my direction. A fleeting expression of irritation crossed his face, but he chose silence over engagement. He continued to inhabit his isolated space, physically close yet emotionally distant, leaving the children and me to navigate the dinner atmosphere alone.

Though brimming with our presence, the table was overshadowed by his noticeable disregard. We endeavored to maintain a semblance of normalcy, yet his absence cast a lingering shadow over our attempts. The following morning, just before heading to church, CW and I had words; as the argument with CW escalated, I found myself calling him stupid in anger. The weight of this act didn't hit me until the children and I were at church.

During my worship, the usually comforting and connecting act of worship felt hollow, as if my offerings of praise were not reaching God. It was then that I realized the Holy Spirit was disciplining me, making me aware of the wrong in my actions from the past day and this morning.

This was a culmination of the disunity that had been growing in our marriage, a disunity that was fueled by our inability to communicate effectively and our constant bickering. Leaving the church in the middle of worship, I returned home with a storm of emotions. My apology to CW was a testament to my striving to be the wife God called me to be. A sincere apology was a step towards mending what had been broken, not just with CW but with God and within myself.

Marriages often face trials and tribulations, but conflicts are managed with gentleness and mutual understanding in a loving marriage. Unfortunately, that wasn't the reality for us for years. Our marriage seemed trapped in a cycle of 'Criticism,' where we would constantly find fault with each other; 'Defensiveness,' where we would protect ourselves from perceived attacks; 'Contempt,' where we would show disrespect and disdain towards each other; and 'Stonewalling,' where we would emotionally withdraw from each other.

These behaviors became unwanted guests in our marriage. Our interactions were often strained, with attacks on each other's character or a lack of responsiveness. These patterns only led to anger and emotional distance. Reflecting on my interactions with CW, I recognized my defensiveness and criticism brought on tribulation in the intimate theater of our marriage, a stage where life's pressures often seemed unbearable.

During another argument with CW, a profound moment of despair where I felt the weight of our disunity, I began to understand the spiritual significance of tribulation in my marriage. Each challenge, every moment of pain, seemed like a relentless pressing, squeezing out the issues hidden in the crevices of my heart. It was a moment of realization, a turning point in my journey of spiritual growth.

This journey led me to a pivotal realization while reading Mark 14:29-72. The story of Peter and the disciples, who vowed to die with Christ yet faltered at a crucial moment, mirrored my spiritual struggles. Their tribulation manifested the weaknesses in their love and faith, much like my marital challenges revealed my spiritual shortcomings.

Reading Mark 14:29-72 opened my eyes to a divine revelation: God was using the tribulations in my marriage to serve a threefold purpose - to Manifest, Mend, and Conform me into the image of His Son.

Tribulation in Transformation

In the intricate journey of life, tribulations act not merely as obstacles but as essential catalysts for growth, mirroring the careful pruning of grapevines or the intense refinement of gold. Though harsh, these processes are purposeful and aim to manifest all that is not like Christ, revealing hidden scars, wholes, and issues that need mending.

This understanding can bring hope, knowing that even amid trials, there is a purpose and a potential for transformation. Tribulation is not a punishment but a tool that God uses to shape us into the image of His Son, Jesus. It's about learning from our mistakes, growing from our challenges, and becoming stronger through trials.

Trials and difficulties can lead to spiritual mending or plunge you into despair. The outcome is not predetermined; it depends on how you respond to them. By recognizing the parts of yourself that do not align with Christ's teachings and allowing God's grace to improve them, you can experience significant personal and spiritual growth.

It's about trusting in God's plan, even when things seem bleak, and relying on His grace to guide you through the storm. It's about understanding that God's grace is not just a concept but a tangible force that can transform our lives if we let it.

The divine purpose behind tribulation is not to cause us suffering but to strip away the nonessential, revealing our true strengths and virtues in Christ Jesus. Like gold purified in fire, we emerge resilient, robust, and valuable from our trials, reflecting Jesus's characteristics. This understanding can foster a sense of gratitude, knowing that our challenges are not in vain but are gifts from God for our spiritual growth.

Manifest

The primary purpose of the tribulation is to draw out from our hearts the unholy aspects, issues, flaws, and sins that reside within our hearts. Jesus' arrest brought to the surface hidden struggles Peter and the disciples were unaware of, such as their fluctuating faith, absence of love, and betrayal by abandonment.

Tribulation revealed the issues in their hearts that they didn't know existed. This process is not unique; it's a universal aspect of spiritual growth, where tribulation acts as a refiner's fire, bringing our inner impurities to the surface.

Mend

The second purpose of tribulation is to mend and reconcile the aspects of our hearts that adversity reveals, aspects that diverge from the path Jesus has taught us. The journey of spiritual mending unfolds as a two-fold process. It requires the healing touch of Jesus' words, which we can find in the scriptures and through prayer, alongside our genuine remorse for the flaw (s) tribulation exposes in our hearts.

This process emphasizes the power of our actions in the transformation process, making us feel empowered and responsible for our growth. It's about acknowledging our shortcomings, seeking forgiveness, and consciously changing our behavior. This intricate and profoundly personal mending process is as much about restoration as discovery. This mending begins with the words of Jesus, serving as the first stitch in mending Peter's broken spirit.

Mark 14:72 captures this pivotal moment: "Immediately, the rooster crowed the second time. Then Peter *remembered Jesus's words:* 'Before the rooster crows twice, you will disown me three times.'

And he broke down and wept." This moment of recollection for Peter, where he remembered Jesus's prophetic words, marked the beginning of his path to healing. The healing process cannot commence without the guiding conviction of God's word through the Holy Spirit. Like the precise work of a skilled surgeon, Jesus' words delicately sewed the initial suture to mend the wounds in Peter's heart. This essential first step, imbued with love and wisdom, lays the foundation for a more profound restoration process, guiding us toward a renewed sense of peace and wholeness. It underscores the critical importance of embedding God's Word in our hearts — the inaugural stitch in the fabric of our healing journey.

The second essential stitch in Jesus' spiritual healing process is our genuine remorse, a profound aspect vividly illustrated in Peter's remorse. His weeping and repentance signify regret and a profound, transformative realization of his sin of desertion, lack of faith, and love for Jesus.

This remorse is vital, for without it, Christ cannot proceed in mending what the tribulation manifested out of our hearts and healing our issues, holes, and spiritual voids within us.

This is emphasized in Proverbs 28:13, which teaches the importance of confessing and renouncing sins to find mercy.

Conform

The third purpose of tribulation is to conform us to the image of Christ. When we embrace genuine remorse and repentance, we become mailable in God's hand, allowing Him to reshape our character in the likeness of Christ, in alignment with His intentions. (Romans 8:29).

Our conformity transforms us to display God's will to be done on earth as in heaven. Through the trials I've faced, I've come to realize profound issues within me, such as a lack of faith and love for God, a struggle to surrender my rights, a failure to submit to CW, low self-esteem, and careless speech.

These revelations, though painful, have been instrumental in my growth. However, my lack of remorse for these manifestations from my heart has hindered my healing, leading me to repeat the same tests, akin to a hamster running endlessly on a wheel. Just as rigorous workouts shape us, the challenges in my marriage have been pivotal in molding me into the likeness of Christ.

Each challenge has presented itself as a test, and I've often found myself repeating it until I let go of my ego and humbly submit myself under the mighty hand of God. This growth process has been slow and continuous, unfolding over three decades of serving God. Each tribulation has sculpted my character, like a sculptor chiseling a marble block into Christ's image.

I endured hardship in the crucible of these trials, mending and conforming. There were many moments when following the right path seemed like an error, as it demanded the relinquishment of my wants, causing profound pain. This paradox of making tough choices to take my cross and deny myself for Christ's sake is common among believers.

It reveals our commitment to Christ and the transformative power of His resurrection. By enduring momentary discomfort for the promise of eternal blessings, we emulate Christ's example and showcase our faith's strength.

Guided by the teachings in 1 Peter 2:18-24, 1 Peter 3:1-4, and Colossians 3:23-24 these became my guiding light, reframing suffering as a divine gift. A gift that no one wants. They encouraged me to perceive tribulations not as burdens but as instruments for spiritual maturation and alignment with Christ's essence.

Armed with this renewed perspective, I learned to navigate marital challenges with patience, humility, and boundless love, intending to do it as unto the Lord.

In this journey, I encountered a spectrum of emotions - doubt, fear, disappointment, sadness, frustration, pride, and, eventually, a peaceful acceptance.

During my marriage's most challenging times, I earnestly prayed for a best friend in the Lord—someone with whom I could share my struggles. However, God seemed to have a different plan, denying my request not out of indifference but with profound foresight.

God knew all too well that if I were given such a companion, I would likely turn to them first rather than Him. Instead of fulfilling my wish for a best friend, God graced me with something unexpectedly beautiful: two rose petals, symbolizing individuals He carefully placed in my life at just the right moments.

These were not the companions I had asked for, but they were the ones I needed — gifts from God to remind me that He is always listening and present and that He alone should be the first refuge for my heart's cries. The first rose petal was my biological sister, Alam Jean, a Christian. Like me, she had weathered the storm of an unequally yoked marriage. Her wisdom experiences provided comfort and perspective.

She constantly reminded me of God's faithfulness and often contrasted CW's demeanor with her departed husband, painting CW in a comparatively favorable light. Her steadfast encouragement was a beacon during a particular time in my marital challenges.

Jackie, a co-worker, was the second rose petal God graced me with. Our bond was instantaneous. Jackie's unparalleled listening skills offered solace. She never interjected with scriptures or unsolicited advice; she listened, providing a sanctuary for my weary heart.

Avoid sharing sensitive details about your marriage with others if it casts your spouse negatively. Also, maintaining confidentiality in marriage means being careful about whom you discuss marital issues with, particularly gossipers. If they gossip to you, they'll gossip about you.

In conclusion, let tribulations be the gardener that cultivates the rich fruits of character and spiritual maturity within us, inspiring us to reach our full potential.

How do repentance and remorse play a crucial role in personal transformation according to the biblical perspective described in the text?

CHAPTER 14

Tracing the Roots of Marital Challenges

Genesis of Desire

My deep yearning for love has been a profound challenge in my marriage. Every woman seeks love, and its absence in a union brings complications.

I reflected on whether my childhood, perhaps the absence of my father, was the reason for this strong desire or whether my mother's struggles influenced this intense craving for love. I sought understanding from God, who is my therapist and counselor. He directed me to Genesis 3:16, which elucidates Eve's consequence following her disobedience. The scripture details, "I will greatly multiply your sorrow and your conception; in pain, you shall bring forth children; your desire shall be for your husband, and he shall rule over you." This verse underscores that part of Eve's retribution was a deep-seated yearning for her husband, encapsulated by the Hebrew word 'tûqâ, signifying an intense longing.

Genesis 3:16, Genesis 4:7, and Song of Solomon 7:10 are the only instances where 'tûqâ' is mentioned, each providing a nuanced understanding of desire.

Scholars' interpretations of Eve's desire in Genesis 3:16 diverge significantly. Some posit that Eve desired to dominate or usurp her husband's authority, drawing parallels with Genesis 4:7, where sin is depicted as lurking, desiring dominion over Cain, yet he is advised to master it.

Conversely, others interpret Eve's desire as a genuine craving for her husband's love, affection, and intimacy, referencing the Song of Solomon 7:10, "I am my beloved's, and his desire is toward me," to support this view. I align with the interpretation that perceives Eve's desire as a deep longing for her husband's love, affection, and intimacy, even amidst the aftermath of childbirth. This interpretation suggests that, despite the pain associated with childbirth as a consequence of her disobedience, Eve now has an inherent desire for her husband's affection and love.

Submission to Adam was Eve's second consequence of her disobedience. Eve's relationship with Adam was altered, transitioning from an equal partnership to a hierarchy where Adam assumes dominion. This shift underscores the directive for wives to submit to their husbands because submission isn't inherent in their DNA.

As I contemplated Paul's guidance for husbands and wives in Ephesians, it led me to question why he emphasized the importance of wives demonstrating submission and respect to their husbands and husbands showing love to their wives without allowing bitterness to take root.

Might Paul's counsel be deeply connected to the fallout from Adam and Eve's transgression? In the wake of Adam's fall, is it possible that men are particularly prone to bitterness that impedes their ability to love their wives fully? Conversely, might women struggle with submission and respect towards their husbands as a response to feeling unloved?

Thus, a wife's desire is not to challenge her husband's authority but to be engulfed in his love. A husband who meets this need for love cultivates a relationship where his wife happily and freely submits to his rule. In the narrative of Eve's disobedience, a significant consequence was passed down through generations of women. It instilled in them an inherent longing for love and affection for their husbands.

This yearning, deeply rooted in women's essence, is not a mere societal construct but something more profound, akin to an element woven into our DNA. At the heart of a wife's yearning lies not a desire to usurp her husband's place of authority but rather a profound longing to be cradled in the warmth of his affection. The foundations of a harmonious partnership are laid within this sanctuary of love.

Feeling cherished and understood, the wife naturally and enthusiastically embraces her role, freely aligning herself with her husband's guidance.

Powered by genuine affection, this give-and-take dance fosters a relationship where leadership and support coexist in beautiful symmetry.

In my marriage, my relentless pursuit of fulfillment through CW ended in disappointment and tension between us. I found myself frequently complaining and criticizing CW for not fulfilling my needs. A need he couldn't fulfill no matter how hard he tried. My cries for love overwhelmed CW.

He felt like a bobblehead nodding to my demands, yet inside, he was crumbling, unsure of how to meet the tsunami of my emotional needs. This constant nodding, absent of accurate understanding or connection, only deepened the chasm of loneliness between us, leaving us both feeling isolated and unfulfilled.

I've realized that when someone withdraws and stops communicating, they often don't believe we're willing to listen, signaling a deep need to shift our approach to communication and understanding. That is precisely what I did.

I sought divine guidance, turning to the Lord with questions about who will love me and how to handle my innate longing for love from my spouse in the absence of? I pondered, how should I overcome this intense longing for love? Inspired by the words of Paul, you have been made complete in Christ. Colossian 2:10b. The Lord enlightened me to realize that completeness is found in Him and Him alone. All the fulfillment I seek resides in His presence. My desire for love won't be eradicated; instead, it will be satisfied through my union with Him.

Colossians 2:10a became a cornerstone of my spiritual journey, offering a profound truth that reshaped my understanding of fulfillment and wholeness. This verse spoke to the depths of my soul, challenging me to seek fulfillment not in my spouse but in Christ alone.

John 6:35 offered another spiritual nourishment and insight. Jesus declared, "I am the bread of life; whoever comes to me shall not hunger, and whoever believes in me shall never thirst."

These words were a balm to my weary heart amid my love hunger. They gave me the answer to fulfilling my deepest hunger and thirst for love, understanding, and connection — which could only be satiated in Jesus. Understanding this has endowed me with the grace to stay and the faith to finish in a marriage where love for me is limited.

When a strong desire to be loved becomes overpowering, I stand and feed off God's strength by repeating John 6:35 and Colossian 2:10b back to Him. While a spouse can provide love, support, and companionship and share joys and challenges, expecting them to meet all of one's emotional, spiritual, and personal growth needs is unrealistic and burdensome.

Recognizing and accepting that your spouse cannot fulfill your deepest needs is crucial for a healthy you. This perspective fosters a stronger bond and mutual respect without the unrealistic expectation of being each other's sole source of fulfillment.

Under God's tutelage on love, He taught me to give love when I sought love. Under His guidance, I am on a journey to understand and embody love and completeness in Him. God illuminated six essential pillars that I speak of in chapter ten in more detail. These have anchored my growth: faith, prayer, applying God's Word, love for God with every aspect of my being, dying to self, and loving myself as God loves me.

These pillars have shaped my understanding of love and fulfillment in Jesus, transforming how I express love, especially when I yearn for love. One tangible example of how God taught me to give love amidst my longing involves my interactions with CW. After CW's stonewalling, I felt a divine nudge, a gentle prompting from the Holy Spirit, to extend kindness towards CW without expecting anything in return.

This task initially felt incredibly daunting, akin to the struggles described in the song, "I'm climbing the rough side of the mountain." My nature resisted; it seemed against every instinct to offer love in moments when I felt deprived of it myself. This selflessness, this "death to self," was challenging yet liberating.

However, obedience to these divine promptings led to a profound transformation within me. Each act of kindness, though initially against the grain of my emotions, became a stepping stone toward personal freedom. God taught me a pivotal lesson: even true love expects something in return: acceptance of its love. It was a practical application of God's Word, embodying the teachings of Jesus, who loved the world unconditionally and served others, even to the point of death.

Yet, God's love expected the 'whosoever' to accept His love for His love to benefit their relationship with Him. But His love wasn't predicated on receiving love; He just loved and wanted me to do so, too.

Moreover, this process helped deepen my love for God with every aspect of my being. Recognizing that every act of kindness was not just towards CW but also an act of worship and obedience to God, I found my actions rooted in a more profound love for God rather than the fleeting emotions of the moment.

Through faith, bolstered by consistent prayer and the daily application of God's Word, I learned to navigate the complexities of human emotions and relationships.

I knew that the foundation of godly love is not in receiving but in giving, not in claiming but in offering, and not in keeping score but in losing count. This transformative journey under God's tutelage on love reshaped my relationship with CW and my understanding of what it means to be truly fulfilled in Christ's completeness.

What lessons can be learned about the nature of true fulfillment in Christ, and how do the six essential pillars—faith, prayer, applying God's Word, loving God wholly, dying to self, and loving oneself as God loves—contribute to finding completeness in Jesus?

CHAPTER 15

The Love Challenge

Loving without expectation of reciprocity is daunting, yet this act reveals divine love's true essence. The challenge lies in overcoming obstacles that teach us how to live authentically. These include experiences of rejection, suffering, deprivation, injustice, personal weaknesses, insults, trials, persecutions, and other hardships.

Through these difficulties, we learn that unconditional love's proper depth and resilience can only be fully realized when we place our faith and trust in God's plan and promises. As we embark on the practical application of agape love, God's kind of love, I invite you to explore the Love Challenges below. I took these steps within my unequally yoked marriage in an earnest attempt to love as God loves—a goal I humbly admit I have yet to attain fully.

Yet, in the striving, I find growth and empowerment to transform as CW witnessed my transformation.

1 Corinthians 12:4-7

4 Love is patient, love is kind and is not jealous; love does not brag and is not arrogant; 5 does not act unbecomingly; it does not seek its own, is not provoked, does not take into account a wrong suffered,

6 does not rejoice in unrighteousness, but rejoices with the truth; 7 bears all things, believes all things, hopes all things, endures all things.

Love Challenge 1:

Patience - Understanding Over Reaction

Spiritual Growth Aspect:

Faith and Loving God with All Your Being

Challenge:

When faced with impatience or harsh words from your spouse, show patience and understanding, reflecting your faith and commitment to loving God with all your being by extending grace.

Act of Love:

Say "I love you" after your spouse displays impatience. This simple yet profound declaration allows you to die to your feelings for Christ's sake.

Scripture: "Be completely humble and gentle; be patient, bearing with one another in love." - Ephesians 4:2

Holistic Impact:

Spirit: Cultivates a spirit of peace and long-suffering.

Soul (Mind): Encourages emotional resilience and empathy, soothing the mind with understanding.

Flesh: Teaches self-control over immediate reactive behaviors.

Love Challenge 2:

Responding to Criticism with Acts of Kindness

Spiritual Growth Aspect:

Applying God's Word

Challenge:

Respond to criticism kindly, applying God's word by turning the other cheek. Instead of taking offense when your spouse criticizes you, express gratitude by saying, "Thank you for the feedback."

Act of Love:

Commit to holding back negative remarks towards your spouse, even negativity. Scripture: "Do not repay evil for evil or reviling for reviling, but on the contrary, bless, for to this you were called, that you may obtain a blessing." - 1 Peter 3:9

Holistic Impact:

Spirit: Enriches your spiritual life with the fruit of the Spirit, kindness.

Soul (Mind): Foster's inner strength and confidence, finding worth in God's love.

Flesh: Challenges natural inclinations to retaliate, promoting gentle actions.

Love Challenge 3:

Transforming Rejection into Acts of Love

Spiritual Growth Aspect:

Death to Self.

Challenge:

Practice acceptance and respond with unconditional love when feeling rejected.

Act of Love:

Meet a need for your spouse without expecting anything in return. Scripture: "But I say to you, love your enemies and pray for those who persecute you." - Matthew 5:44

Holistic Impact:

Spirit: Embodies Christ's unconditional love.

Soul (Mind): Heals the wounds of rejection, bringing joy and fulfillment.

Flesh: Overcomes the tendency to withdraw, performing tangible acts of love.

Love Challenge 4:

Fostering Humility in Disagreements with a Gesture of Love

Spiritual Growth Aspect:

Loving God with All Your Being

Challenge:

Embrace humility and seek to understand your spouse's perspective during disagreements.

Act of Love:

During a disagreement, pause and offer a gesture of love by holding your spouse's hands, looking into their eyes, and calmly stating, "Let's approach this with understanding and love for each other."

Scripture: "With all humility and gentleness, with patience, bearing with one another in love." - Ephesians 4:2

Holistic Impact:

Spirit: Aligns our spirit with God's, experiencing divine grace.

Soul (Mind): Reduces emotional turmoil, enhancing peace.

Flesh: Encourages physical expressions of reconciliation.

Love Challenge 5:

Embracing Forgiveness and Letting Go of Wrongs

Spiritual Growth Aspect:

Loving Yourself as God Loves You

Challenge:

Choose forgiveness in misunderstandings, reflecting on God's forgiveness.

Act of Love:

Apologize sincerely over a favorite meal, expressing your commitment to change. Enjoy a day of your spouse's preferred activities, symbolizing forgiveness and a fresh start. Scripture: "Be kind to one another, tenderhearted, forgiving one another, as God in Christ forgave you." - Ephesians 4:32.

Holistic Impact:

Spirit: Purifies our spirit through forgiveness.

Soul (Mind): It liberates from past hurts and fosters peace. Flesh: It promotes warm, loving actions despite hurt.

Love Challenge 6:

Transforming Suffering with Grace

Spiritual Growth Aspect:

Loving God with All Your Being

Challenge:

Respond to hardship gracefully, seeing it as an opportunity to demonstrate your love for God and your spouse.

Act of Love:

Ask your spouse to pray with you instead of taking offense when disappointed. If you've neglected responsibilities, openly admit it, citing biblical guidance. Thank them for their patience and the chance to improve, expressing love with a hug. If your spouse errs without apologizing, pray for grace to handle it in a way that honors God and your marriage. Scripture: "But he said to me, 'My grace is sufficient for you, for my power is made perfect in weakness.'" - 2 Corinthians 12:9

Holistic Impact:

Spirit: Draws closer to God through shared experiences of suffering and comfort.

Soul (Mind): Builds resilience and hope, finding strength in trials.

Flesh: Teaches discipline and endurance in the face of discomfort.

Love Challenge 7:

Cultivating Respect in Disagreements

Spiritual Growth Aspect:

Applying God's Word Scripture: "Let your speech always be gracious, seasoned with salt, so that you may know how you ought to answer each person." - Colossians 4:6

Challenge:

Show respect, seek understanding during disagreements, and apply God's Word to resolve conflicts.

Act of Love:

After a disagreement, express admiration for an aspect of your spouse's perspective. Write a note titled "I Love You Because," and list three qualities or actions that make you love them, detailing each. Scripture: "Do nothing from selfish ambition or conceit, but in humility count others more significant than yourselves." - Philippians 2:3

Holistic Impact:

Spirit: Enhances spiritual maturity by recognizing that my spouse is made in God's image.

Soul (Mind): Improves emotional intelligence, valuing another's perspective.

Flesh: Controls our physical responses to reflect respect and understanding.

Love Challenge 8:

Prioritizing 'Us' Over 'Me'

Spiritual Growth Aspect:

Death to Self

Challenge:

Make decisions that benefit the relationship, reflecting the concept of dying to self.

Act of Love:

1. Decide to uplift and cherish your spouse more than usual.
2. Start by listening with greater attention and avoid interrupting them.
3. Show your partner that you value their perspective.

Scripture: "Do nothing from selfish ambition or conceit, but in humility count others more significant than yourselves." - Philippians 2:3.

Holistic Impact:

Spirit: Fosters unity and partnership, reflecting God's desire for our relationships.

Soul (Mind): Fulfills the longing for connection, enhancing a sense of belonging.

Flesh: Challenges selfish desires, prompting actions that benefit the relationship.

Love Challenge 9:

Choosing Peace Over Pettiness

Spiritual Growth Aspect:

Loving Yourself as God Loves

Challenge:

Choose understanding and peace in moments of irritation, reflecting on God's forgiveness.

Act of Love:

In moments of upset with your spouse, extend a token of love through a thoughtful deed on their behalf. This act of kindness overcomes personal grievances and embodies humility. Carry out this gesture as if you were doing it for the Lord, mindful that your spouse, if angry, might not immediately appreciate it. Share a peaceful moment to reconnect and prioritize peace. Scripture: "If it is possible, as far as it depends on you, live at peace with everyone." - Romans 12:18

Holistic Impact:

Spirit: Cultivates a spirit of peace, aligning with the Prince of Peace.

Soul (Mind): Soothes and calms the mind, enhancing emotional wellness.

Flesh: Encourages physical restraint from petty reactions, teaching us to embody peace.

Love Challenge 10:

Embracing Submission to Your Husband

Spiritual Growth Aspect:

Loving God with All Your Being

Challenge:

When your spouse wants to do something that isn't sinful but doesn't make sense, practice biblical submission as an act of faithfulness and love in your marriage.

Act of Love:

Discuss and act on ways to support each other's roles in the marriage. Once a month, prepare an appreciation dinner for your spouse as a token of appreciation, simply out of love. Scripture: "Wives, submit to your husbands, as is fitting in the Lord." - Colossians 3:18.

Holistic Impact:

Spirit: Strengthens spiritual submission to God, understanding His design for marriage.

Soul (Mind): Encourages trust and vulnerability, deepening the emotional bond. Flesh: Promotes supportive actions, overcoming personal pride and societal norms.

Love Challenge 11:

Embracing Sacrifice in Love

Spiritual Growth Aspect:

Death to Self

Challenge:

Actively look for ways to sacrifice your needs for your partner, embodying profound love.

Act of Love:

Give up something personal for your spouse's needs or desires. Scripture: "Greater love has no one than this, that someone lay down his life for his friends." - John 15:13.

Holistic Impact:

Spirit: Mirrors Christ's sacrificial love, deepening our spiritual connection.

Soul (Mind): Brings joy and fulfillment through selfless acts, enriching the soul.

Flesh: Teaches the body to let go of personal desires, embodying the essence of sacrifice.

Love Challenge 12:

Prayer Challenge: Integrating Prayer into Every Aspect of Your Relationship

Spiritual Growth Aspect:

Prayer

Challenge: Recognize prayer as key for managing marriage's highs and lows.

Act of Prayer: Start praying today for your spouse's heart, focusing on three areas where you hope to see God's influence in their life and your marriage. **Scripture:** "And this is the confidence that we have toward him, that if we ask anything according to his will, he hears us." - 1 John 5:14.

Holistic Impact:

Spirit: Deepens your spiritual connection, fostering a shared faith journey.

Soul (Mind): Promotes emotional intimacy and communication, building trust and understanding through shared spiritual practices.

Flesh: Bring physical closeness as you come together in prayer, reinforcing the physical expression of your spiritual bond.

Love Challenge 13:

Faith Challenge: Trusting Beyond Sight

Spiritual Growth Aspect:

Faith

Challenge: Trust God's plan and promises for your life and relationship, particularly during hard times. Embody faith to show trust in His sovereignty and love.

Act of Love: Serve your spouse emotionally daily. Say good morning, don't go to bed angry, thank God for them daily, and make them feel safe. If they let you in, focus on getting to know your spouse better in areas you've rarely discussed. Be quick to listen, forgive, and love your spouse. Scripture: "For we live by faith, not by sight." - 2 Corinthians 5:7.

Holistic Impact:

Spirit: Reinforces your spiritual foundation, deepening your relationship with God through trust and reliance on His guidance.

Soul (Mind): Cultivates a sense of peace and hope as the mind learns to focus on God's faithfulness rather than life's uncertainties.

Flesh: Challenges the natural inclination to rely solely on what is seen and understood, encouraging actions that demonstrate trust in God's unseen plans.

The Love Challenge was a divine experiment that transformed my love for CW. Initially, loving him as God loves me seemed impossible, as I lacked that depth of love. However, I embraced agape love through gratefulness for God's love for me. Until I grew to love God more than myself and surrender my will to God, I could not love CW with agape love. When I allowed Christ to close the casket lid of my flesh and stopped resisting, love began to bloom.

No matter the tensions or the mood lingering from the previous day, I committed each day to acts of love. These were not just to counter my rejection or curb my quick-to-offend emotions but to affirm my unwavering support and love for CW.

In moments of silence or strain, I clung to the teachings of Matthew 5:44—choosing to love, bless, do good, and pray.

This approach was how I learned to navigate and overcome the challenges in our relationship, seeing each act of love as a step closer to embodying the love Christ gives me.

Following God's direction in showing CW love despite our relationship's challenges often made me feel foolish, vulnerable, and naive.

I wrestled with doubts: Was this truly God speaking to me? Yet, as I persevered, I began to see these actions not as signs of weakness but as demonstrations of strength and obedience.

Embracing this vulnerability allowed me to open up to the transformative power of God's love. It taught me that true strength often requires the courage to love without reservations or conditions, reflecting the sacrificial love that Jesus exemplified.

I was also seeking to experience the profound peace described in Scripture—the peace of God that surpasses all understanding, which is promised if I walked in His ways (Philippians 4:7).

In my pursuit, I longed to deepen my knowledge of Christ—not just His power but also the fellowship of His sufferings, being conformed to His likeness even unto death (Philippians 3:10).

In these moments of obedience—choosing to love despite my feelings—I discovered a profound sense of God's peace, a peace that transformed me.

These love challenges imparted priceless wisdom: love is a deliberate choice. It's not merely an emotion but a conscious decision to die to self to bring God glory, even in the most challenging times.

This approach drew me closer to understanding God's will. It revolutionized my interactions with CW. I was striving to anchor my actions in a love that mirrors the depth and commitment Christ calls us to embody.

What will applying the principles of 'agape love' in your unequally yoked marriage lead you to do?

CHAPTER 16

Staying the Course When It's Hard

In the furnace of an unequally yoked marriage, the flames of triggers, pain, rejection, judgment, and weariness often burn intensely. Yet, within these searing experiences, the opportunity for profound spiritual growth emerges.

This chapter delves into how such emotional trials have not only tested my faith but have become unexpected conduits for deepening my relationship with God, enhancing my prayer life, and earnestly applying His Word to every aspect of my existence. As I navigate these challenges, I am learning to love God with all my heart, die to myself, and embrace God's love for me, transforming my trials into faith triumphs.

Triggers: The Spark of Self-Discovery

My journey to understand and overcome my emotional triggers has been profoundly transformative. The turning point came at a women's conference where I learned what a trigger was.

A speaker there shared her experience with emotional triggers within her marriage, revealing how her husband's actions would unexpectedly affect her feelings.

This idea of 'triggers' was a revelation to me; it was the key to understanding the emotional turmoil I had been experiencing. I felt a mix of emotions and relief as I finally had a name for what I was going through, and I also felt a sense of urgency to start my journey of self-discovery and healing.

Recognizing these triggers was like discovering a hidden power, each revelation a step towards mastering my relationship's complex dynamics. Upon returning home, fueled by newfound clarity, I embarked on a mission to identify and understand the triggers that disrupted my emotional balance.

This was not about assigning blame but discerning the patterns that precipitated my distress. In the narrative of managing my triggers, a crucial step was recognizing what specifically triggered my emotional responses.

Initially, when I shared my feelings or concerns with my husband, his tendency to briefly acknowledge and then quickly return to his activities left me feeling unheard and invalidated.

Over time, I began to notice a pattern: this type of interaction consistently led to heightened emotional distress and subsequent arguments. This recurring pattern of distress after specific behaviors indicated that these were not just frustrating moments but significant triggers.

Reflecting on these repeated emotional experiences made me realize the root of my reaction—my deep-seated need for validation and the feeling of being disregarded.

Recognizing these triggers was pivotal. I then communicated this understanding with my husband, explaining the importance of feeling acknowledged and requesting changes in communication.

This realization allowed me to approach our interactions with more clarity and purpose, leading to constructive changes in our communication.

Additionally, I started to check if it was a good time for me to talk, respecting his space and time. I also prepared myself emotionally before these discussions by role-playing potential responses and aligning my actions with Biblical teachings, reminding myself that 'anger is a trait of a fool,' and I no longer wanted to embody that trait.

Incorporating these changes into my interactions and effectively identifying and addressing my triggers improved how I responded to my husband and allowed me to write the outcome of my story.

It also deepened my trust and reliance on prayer for wisdom in managing my emotional responses. Prayer was a source of strength and guidance, helping me stay calm and focused during difficult conversations.

The journey to overcome my triggers was not about eliminating them but learning how to become proactive and not reacting. It was a path of self-discovery, healing, and empowerment. Understanding my triggers allowed me to navigate my emotions with greater awareness and control.

This process has been challenging but incredibly rewarding, leading me to a stronger, more peaceful version of myself.

PAIN: The Teacher of Conformity

Pain respects no one; it is a universal experience that transcends all barriers of identity and circumstance.

It thrusts us into profound realms of questioning and introspection, touching every life without prejudice.

Pain is the gift no one wants, yet it's the most profound teacher. I have come to see it as an unexpected yet profound teacher. Pain catalyzes growth and conformity. It enters our lives under divine oversight, approved by God for reasons that may not be immediately clear.

The Book of Job in the Bible is a profound exploration of pain and suffering and how humans understand their relationship with God in the face of immense personal tragedy.

Job, a wealthy and pious man, experiences catastrophic losses, including wealth, children, and health. Despite his severe hardships, Job maintains his faith, although he struggles to understand the reasons for his suffering.

The purpose behind God allowing Job to endure such pain and hardship is multifaceted. It tests and ultimately strengthens Job's faith, demonstrating his righteousness and unwavering trust in God despite his circumstances.

Additionally, the story illustrates the limitations of human understanding regarding divine wisdom and the nature of suffering.

It challenges the notion that earthly suffering is always a direct consequence of personal sin and highlights the complexity of God's plan and the importance of faith in the face of the inexplicable.

The Bible's profound wisdom and transformative power have been invaluable guides for me during pain and uncertainty. For instance, during a particularly challenging period, such as being betrayed by a close friend's kiss.

I found solace in Romans 5:3-5: "We also glory in our sufferings, because we know that suffering produces perseverance; perseverance, character; and character, hope."

And James 1:2-4 encourages believers to "count it all joy" when facing various trials, knowing that the testing of faith develops perseverance. How do you "count it all joy" when in immense pain? This is a challenging concept to embrace, but it's deeply rooted in the belief that such hardships serve a greater purpose in one's spiritual growth and character development.

What was helpful for me when in pain is that I shifted my perspective off of myself to God and stood on His promises, such as Jeremiah 29:11 (KJV): For I know the thoughts that I think toward you, saith the Lord, thoughts of peace, and not of evil, to give you an expected end. Standing on His promises and feeding off His strength, His Word, I could "count it all joy" because I learned that my expected end would be more beneficial than the current pain.

I have earnestly sought God, yearning for a faith as steadfast as Job's amidst severe trials and inexplicable hardships.

I aspire to understand and share the kind of sufferings Paul describes—enduring weariness, pain, frequent vigils, hunger, thirst, and exposure to the elements (2 Corinthians 6:5-10).

But above all, I deeply desire to know Christ more intimately—to experience the power of His resurrection and the fellowship of His sufferings, embracing even the aspects that mirror Christ's path to crucifixion.

These types of pain, trials, and hardships are not simply about enduring pain; they involve engaging with it deeply, questioning it, and ultimately growing from it. They are gateways to deeper faith and closer communion with God as they refine and shape us in His service.

Job, Paul, and Jesus's experiences have taught me that faith can involve lament, questioning, and seeking understanding from God. They have also shown me that pain and suffering are parts of life, even for the righteous who suffer without apparent cause.

This insight led me to view life's challenges as moments where God asks Satan, 'Have you noticed my servant, Sister Grateful?' This new way of thinking has fundamentally changed how I approach life's trials, making me more mindful that suffering and pain must go through God's hand of approval.

It's not that God causes our suffering, but He allows it to refine our faith and character for a greater purpose. This ultimately requires a profound trust in God's sovereignty and wisdom.

From Job, Paul, and Jesus's experiences, I gleaned several steps to navigate through times of pain:

1. **Uphold Faith in God:** In the face of suffering, commit steadfastly never to curse God and to trust in His sovereignty, even when understanding seems elusive. As Job 13:15 reminds us, 'Though he slay me, yet will I hope in him.

2. **Seek Understanding Through Prayer**: Consistently seek God's presence for comfort, guidance, and deeper understanding, worshiping Him as sovereign. James 1:5 encourages this, "If any of you lacks wisdom, you should ask God, who gives generously to all without finding fault, and it will be given to you."

3. **Embrace Humility**: Recognizing your limited understanding of God's plans is critical, as stated in Proverbs 11:2, "When pride comes, then comes disgrace, but with humility comes wisdom."

4. **Practice Patience and Resilience**: Understand that pain serves a purpose and requires patience and resilience, waiting for God's timing. Romans 5:3-4 supports this, "Not only so, but we also glory in our sufferings, because we know that suffering produces perseverance; perseverance, character; and character, hope."

5. **Engage in Honest Dialogue with God**: Being honest with God about your feelings deepens the relationship and aids healing, as modeled in many of David's psalms, like Psalm 62:8, 'Trust in him at all times, you people; pour out your hearts to him, for God is our refuge.' This open and honest dialogue with God fosters a sense of trust and deepens our relationship with Him.

6. **Value the Support of the Church**: Continue attending church for encouragement and prayer support during difficult times. Hebrews 10:25 advises, "Not giving up meeting together, as some are in the habit of doing, but encouraging one another—and all the more as you see the Day approaching."

7. **Cultivate an Eternal Perspective**: Live for the next world; you will gain this one. Live with an eye on eternity, prioritizing your relationship with God over earthly concerns. Colossians 3:2 says, "Set your minds on things above, not earthly things."

8. **Recognize God's Redemptive Power**: Take heart that God can redeem your pain for a greater purpose and restore what has been lost or broken, as illustrated in Romans 8:28, "And we know that in all things God works for the good of those who love him, who have been called according to his purpose."

In the intricate dance of life, where pain and purpose are interwoven, Job's story is a beacon of hope, reminding us that our fierce trials are never purposeless.

Through the lens of faith, patience, and humility, I learned to navigate the storms of life, not as a victim of my circumstance but as a seeker of a deeper communion with God.

How have your challenges deepened your understanding of suffering and redemption, and how has this shaped your relationship with God?

Rejection: The Refiner of Identity

The specter of rejection was a haunting melody in my life. For years, the emotional withdrawal and rejection from CW felt like a personal failure, deeply wounding my self-esteem. Unlike physical injuries, the scars of emotional wounds are not visible—they cannot be quickly addressed or bandaged.

However, my faith and understanding of God's love for me became a beacon of hope, helping me reshape this rejection experience into a pathway of learning that my happiness and completeness do not depend on another person.

Understanding CW's Rejection

Reflecting on the past, I now understand why CW rejected me. When we first met, his life was in turmoil. I momentarily filled a void he was desperately trying to fill. His attraction to me was based on convenience; I had no children and lived alone, offering an uncomplicated option during his chaotic phase.

However, he never had a genuine soul connection—his interactions were primarily physical, lacking the deeper emotional or spiritual bonds that form lasting relationships. After I embraced my faith, the rejection followed—a predictable outcome given our spiritual misalignment.

At the time, I didn't understand that it wasn't me he was rejecting, but rather the Jesus within me. This realization didn't come quickly, but it was profound.

For years, his rejection was a deep wound, a personal blow. However, after a family gathering, it led me to a profound revelation about my identity. In a moment of vulnerability, CW openly shared his feelings, or lack thereof, in front of a group. This incident inadvertently led me to understand my identity through the gospel's transformative power.

I delve into the full details of this experience in Chapter Nine, the incident that changed the game. It was a transformative moment that shifted my focus from seeking validation from others to finding my strength in Christ.

Each rejection I've faced has been an opportunity to stand firm in the liberation I've found in the gospel of Christ, a reminder of my divine liberation and strength in Jesus. My faith, now more resilient than ever, serves as an unwavering anchor through life's stormy seas, constantly affirming that I am fully equipped to overcome rejection.

Prescription for Overcoming Rejection

Overcoming rejection requires a holistic approach that involves God's grace, spiritual healing, self-awareness, and emotional resilience. This guide offers a structured spiritual prescription for navigating and healing from the pain of rejection, using specific scriptures and reflective practices to cultivate inner strength and renewal.

1. Identity & Self-Worth Boost Prescription

- **Scripture**: Psalm 139:14 & I John 3:1
- **Daily Dose**: Read once daily and reflect on your unique creation.
- **Method**: Acknowledge your wonderfully made and inherent value.
- **Duration**: Continuous for best results.
- **Note**: Use this verse to remind yourself of your significance and worth.

2. Rejection Overcomer Prescription

- **Scripture**: Isaiah 54:10 & 1 Peter 2:9
- **Dosage**: Read and meditate on these verses whenever feelings of rejection surface.
- **Method**: Remind yourself of God's unfailing love and that no one can stand against you if God is for you.
- **Duration**: As needed, to heal and overcome feelings of rejection.
- **Note**: Embrace the promise of God's unwavering support and care as a foundation for healing from rejection.

3. Faith Strengthening Prescription

- **Scripture**: Isaiah 41:10 & Hebrews 13:5

- **Daily Dose**: Reflect on these scriptures to nourish and fortify your faith.
- **Method**: Practice faith by trusting God's promises when life seems unfair.
- **Duration**: Regularly, for continuous growth and reinforcement of your faith.
- **Note**: Daily, engage with God's Word to cultivate a strong, unshakeable faith.

4. *Obedience Enhancement Prescription*

- **Scripture**: John 14:15
- **Daily Dose**: Reflect daily on the connection between love and obedience.
- **Method**: Implement the teachings into daily actions and decisions.
- **Duration**: Ongoing for continuous spiritual alignment.
- **Note**: Strengthen your love and devotion through faithful adherence to Jesus's teachings.

5. *Spiritual Nourishment Prescription*

- **Scripture**: Matthew 4:4
- **Daily Dose**: Meditate on this verse daily to feed your spirit.
- **Method**: Absorb the word of God as spiritual sustenance.
- **Duration**: Continuous for enduring spiritual health.

- **Note**: Embrace Scripture as essential to life, not just physical bread.

6. Sufficiency Capsules Prescription

- **Scripture**: 2 Corinthians 12:9–10
- **Daily Dose**: Reflect on these verses to strengthen faith in Christ's sufficiency.
- **Method**: Internalize the message of divine strength in weakness.
- **Duration**: Regularly reinforced trust in Christ's provision.
- **Note:** Let this Scripture affirm that your weakness provokes God's grace.

7. Emotional Liberation Prescription

- **Scripture**: Luke 4:18
- **Dosage**: Use this verse as required for comfort and freedom.
- **Method**: Reflect on Christ's promises for healing and liberation in His presence.
- **Duration**: Use when needed for ongoing spiritual renewal and freedom.
- **Note**: Let this passage affirm your journey toward healing and breaking free from bondage.

8. Anti-Negativity Medication Prescription

- **Scripture**: 1 Corinthians 13:1-4

- **Daily Dose**: Apply daily love towards self and others.
- **Method**: Use love as a remedy against anger, bitterness, and resentment.
- **Duration**: Consistently for ongoing positivity and emotional health.
- **Note**: Allow the principles of love described in these verses to transform negative emotions into positive actions and feelings.

9. Self-Esteem Mirror Exercise Prescription

- **Scriptures**: Psalm 139:14 & Ephesians 2:10
- **Dosage**: Twice daily, morning and evening.
- **Method**: Stand before a mirror and affirm your value and beauty in Christ.
- **Duration**: Until no longer needed.
- **Note**: Use these affirmations to reinforce your understanding of your worth and purpose in Christ.

10. Completeness Pill Prescription

- **Scripture**: Colossians 2:10b, John 6:35
- **Dosage**: Meditate on these passages to affirm your wholeness in Jesus.
- **Method**: Remind yourself daily of your completeness in Him, lacking nothing.
- **Duration**: Continuously, for a steady recognition of your fulfillment in Jesus Christ.

- **Note**: This practice cultivates awareness of your completeness in Christ, fostering fulfillment and self-sufficiency in your spiritual journey.

This guide offers spiritual support and practical strategies to help individuals to defeat rejection. Relying on the power of God's grace amid rejection, understanding your identity in Christ, renewing your mind through the word of God, and engaging in these reflective practices will transform rejection into personal growth and healing, causing you to conquer rejection.

What methods have you found effective for harnessing inner strength amid rejection, and how have these contributed to your journey toward healing?

Judgment: Embracing Grace Over Judgment

The Modern Echoes of Job's Friends

Experiencing a profound transformation, I've found solace in refraining from allowing others to pass judgment on me. This healing journey echoes an age-old tale of a man named Job and his friends. They, too, sat with him, judging and offering unsolicited opinions on the reasons behind his immense suffering. (Job 2:11-13)

Today, the spirit of Job's friends persists, often manifesting as distant observers peering through the window, eager to decipher internal struggles and confidence in their ability to resolve them. These contemporary 'Job's friends' take on various forms—from well-meaning believers and friends to the sermons of religious leaders and even strangers on the internet—all readily dispensing unsolicited advice and judgments.

I have had many interactions with people who are like Job's friends—preachers and fellow believers who imply that a believer's spiritual shortcomings are why their unsaved spouse has not committed to Jesus. Although these people have good intentions, their judgment and unsolicited advice are only sometimes helpful. One fellow believer once pointed to 1 Peter 3:1-6, suggesting my failure to embody these scriptures in my unequally yoked marriage was why my husband wasn't saved.

These encounters have underscored the importance of recognizing that while advice can be helpful, proper understanding and direction are found through a personal relationship with God. Each spiritual journey is unique and should be respected.

In his letters, Paul adds another layer to the theme of judgment, explicitly cautioning against judging prematurely. In Corinthians 4:5, he advises, "Therefore judge nothing before the appointed time; wait until the Lord comes."

This reminds us that our human judgment is often flawed and incomplete, and true discernment comes only with God's revelation. As believers in Christ, we must acknowledge that not living by our beliefs will lead others to disdain or dismiss faith in Jesus, a concept emphasized in Romans 2:24 (which speaks about how the name of God is blasphemed among the Gentiles because of His people's actions.)

Once, I was convinced that I would never embrace Christianity, mainly due to the discouraging behavior of a self-proclaimed believer. This individual not only indulged in gossip and superficial judgment, like critiquing others for wearing makeup but also acted hypocritically, even engaging in fornication.

Their actions, coupled with the judgmental attitudes of other believers, deeply disheartened me. However, despite their negative influence, God saved me and worked a profound change in my heart. This experience taught me a powerful lesson: no human action can stop the divine act of salvation, which rests solely in God's hands.

It's crucial to remember that our actions, whether good or bad, do not hold the power to determine anyone's salvation.

Salvation is a divine gift from God, bestowed by His grace, and not dependent on anyone's deeds, as clearly stated in Ephesians 2:8-9 (which emphasizes the role of grace in salvation).

My positive or negative deeds do not hold power over my husband's salvation. This realization freed me from the false judgment and opinion of others in my deeds to prevent my husband's salvation, allowing me to distance myself from undue judgment and relieving my husband's burden of blame cast by opinions reminiscent of Job's friends.

The conclusion of Job's story showcases a profound act of empathy orchestrated by God. After enduring his friends' misguided counsel, God instructs Job to pray for them (Job 42:10).

This inspired me to shift my focus off the pain of others judging me, to intercede for them, and to trust in the transformative power of grace and redemption. Choosing grace over judgment draws us closer to God and carves a pathway of healing and liberation from human opinion.

How does facing judgment and unsolicited advice, much like Job endured from his friends, inform your ability to extend grace and empathy to others?

Weariness

Navigating through marital weariness has often felt like enduring an endless ascent. Each challenge seemed to test my spirit, mind, and body, yet it taught me profound lessons in faith, prayer, perseverance, and love.

On a particularly trying day, I was engulfed by a level of weariness previously unknown to me. It was a weariness born from words unspoken, touches unshared, and dreams unraveled thread by thread. I realized that something had to change in our marriage. My cry for connection was at its end. After sharing my feelings with my husband, CW, his vacant gaze reminded me of a cow looking at a passing train—a stark sign of our growing disconnection.

"CW, it feels like we're in a silent movie," I said, trying to bridge the gap with words. "Remember how vibrant our passion used to be?"

Heavy with unspoken conflicts, his silence felt like an insurmountable barrier—a silence marked by the quiet erosion of weariness for me. The lack of CW communication in our home caused the walls to be built higher than the ones that held our roof. I longed to breach the distance and find a riverbed that could lead us back to each other, but each attempt felt like casting stones into a deep, never hearing it land.

Expectations I hadn't realized I harbored were dashed quietly, day by day. I expected partnership, a shared journey where burdens were halved, and joys doubled. Instead, I found myself walking a path littered with the debris of unmet hopes, carrying the weight of our world on my shoulders alone. The constant imbalance depleted reserves with little replenishment.

One evening, I turned to CW, the quiet of the room wrapping around us. "Do you feel like we're living parallel lives?" I asked, hoping to draw him into a deeper connection. CW seemed calm, almost detached. "I think everything's fine," he said, suggesting he felt satisfied with our relationship. This contrasted sharply with my longing and unmet needs, particularly the need to feel loved and truly united as one.

"I often feel quite weary," I confessed, the words heavy with the unspoken. It seems like if I don't start our conversations or come where you are at, you act as though you live alone in this marriage."

But now, his typical silence seemed to reverberate with the echoes of our unresolved issues. It was as though a mask of indifference hid the true extent of our disconnect. The barrier that had formed was intangible but unmistakably present, making each day feel like an uphill struggle. Reaching out to him felt increasingly like grasping at air, a crushing reminder of the void between us.

The stark disparity between our efforts and what we received in return turned the concept of 'us' into a myth. When I tried to delve into these deeper issues, CW would shut down or dismissively say, "You've got it good; you only think of yourself," effectively ending the conversation. His responses left me to confront the painful silence alone, which seemed filled with the echoes of unresolved conflicts.

I couldn't pinpoint what it was, for it was hidden behind a mask of indifference. The weight of constantly reaching out but grasping only emptiness was crushing. Amid this struggle, a friend invited me to her church. The preacher's message from Galatians 6:9 resonated deeply with me: "Let us not become weary in doing good, for at the proper time we will reap a harvest if we do not give up." This verse struck a chord, reminding me of the power of persistence and redirecting my focus to Christ.

At that moment, a sense of peace washed over me, reassuring me that I wasn't alone in my struggles. Encouraged by this newfound clarity, I returned to my marriage with renewed determination. Instead of focusing solely on what I was not receiving, I shifted my perspective and chose to find the good in my marriage. Though seemingly small, this shift was a monumental step in staying the course when I wanted to give up.

While the challenges of one-sidedness did not disappear, my changed attitude brought a newfound sense of patience, dependence on God, and peace inside me to see what the end would be. This experience taught me that overcoming weariness requires more than just perseverance. It demands a resilient spirit fueled by faith and determination.

In Luke 18:1, Jesus exemplifies the importance of persistent prayer. He urges us to keep seeking even when the odds seem stacked against us.

Similarly, in Galatians 6:9 and 2 Thessalonians 3:13, Paul emphasizes the significance of endurance in doing good and not growing weary. What should you do when weariness becomes overwhelming? Here's what you can do, guided by Luke 18:1, Galatians 6:9, and 2 Thessalonians 3:13:

1. **Persist in Prayer** (Luke 18:1): Keep communicating with God through prayer. This constant connection helps maintain your spiritual strength and ensures you don't lose heart when your emotions run wild.
2. **Don't Grow Weary in Doing Good** (Galatians 6:9): Continue to act with kindness and perseverance, knowing that your efforts will harvest righteousness if you do not give up. Approach your good deeds with grace, as though each act were performed for Jesus himself. Such commitment will bring rewards not only in this life but also in the life to come.
3. **Continue to Do What is Right** (2 Thessalonians 3:13): Despite feeling discouraged, maintain your commitment to doing good. This steadfastness is crucial in overcoming spiritual fatigue and finding renewal.

By persisting in prayer, not growing weary of doing good, and continually doing what is right, you can combat spiritual weariness and find renewed strength and hope.

To achieve this, do everything as if you are doing it unto Christ, which shifts your focus away from yourself and towards serving a greater purpose. Remember, God will reward you at His appointed time, so keep that assurance in your soul.

How can you apply the principles of persistent prayer, perseverance in doing good, and unwavering commitment to righteousness to overcome weariness in your own life?

CHAPTER 17

Hearing the Heart

In an unequally yoked marriage, aligning on spiritual and emotional fronts will not happen, leading to a landscape filled with misunderstandings and discord.

Yet, by embracing the disciplines of listening, harnessing the power of words thoughtfully, engaging in constructive venting, setting clear boundaries, and practicing forgiveness — critical elements of what I term "Hearing the Heart" — we can begin to navigate these challenges.

These practices will not solve all our differences, but they have the power to manage conflicts, foster peace, and enhance mutual respect.

This narrative is a testament to my challenges in marriage and how mastering these communication strategies, setting boundaries, and forgiving have provided stability and understanding amidst our spiritual disparities.

The Heart of Listening

Learning to listen — truly listen — has been challenging and complex, yet I continue to strive to listen. The art of active listening transformed my approach to communication, especially in my relationship with CW. I learned to look beyond the surface of spoken words, trying to grasp the underlying emotions and intentions.

This ability became crucial, especially when his words were laced with frustration. Initially, his manner of expression led me to react defensively and dismissively, even when his points were valid, until I learned to listen more deeply and let go of my ego.

In our conversations, I adopted a strategy to help prevent knee-jerk reactions. At the slightest sign of an argument brewing, I would pray silently, take a deep breath, avoid reacting defensively, and instead focus on genuinely hearing what CW was trying to communicate.

Even when his words came out steeped in accusation, I reminded myself to look for the underlying message.

A pivotal moment came just after I returned from a trip. CW shared a personal story. It was rare for him to open up like this, so I knew it must have been significant. He told me about a moment of overwhelming stress he experienced involving a couple of people who had pushed him to his limits.

In search of relief, CW had reached out to Jerry for some marijuana, hoping it would ease his mind. What he hadn't anticipated was the stark difference in potency between the marijuana we used to smoke and the strains available today. After just a couple of puffs, he became incredibly sick, convinced he was on the brink of death. Unable to function, he spent the entire day laid out on the sofa, utterly incapacitated.

As he narrated his ordeal, laughter filled the room. It was a moment of shared amusement until, without much thought, I responded in a way that now haunts me with regret. I told CW he was moving backward in life, and then I began preaching about Jesus, telling him that if he gave his life to Him, he wouldn't need to smoke "reefer" to calm his nerves; Jesus would if he trusted in Him.

The atmosphere shifted, and I saw a change in CW's demeanor—a look that screamed, "I wish I hadn't told her anything." My words, intended to guide, had instead shut him down. I failed to listen, to truly hear CW's vulnerability and need for support.

Reflecting on that moment, I understood that my failure to listen contributed significantly to CW's emotional withdrawal from me throughout our marriage, rooted in my tendency to offer unsolicited advice instead of listening and empathizing.

As I continued to learn to listen, I realized:

- I need to set aside my ego and hold back my responses.
- Before sharing my side, allow my emotions to settle.
- To pause, then ask if CW was open to hearing my thoughts before giving my thoughts. This approach helped avoid immediate, emotionally charged rebuttals.
- CW's weakness is shutting down on complex issues and not knowing how to express himself without sounding angry, anxious, or accusing.
- To respond with empathy rather than counterarguments. This didn't mean suppressing my views but choosing a moment when we were more receptive.

- Like a pinball game that requires two players to keep going, I learned that arguments need fuel from both sides to escalate.
- When CW was in a particular mood, his perception became his reality, irrespective of my words or deeds.
- Effective communication involves more than just exchanging information; it's about recognizing emotions, intentions, and unspoken needs.

The realization that listening is not a guaranteed pathway to closeness has equipped me with the skills to navigate the complexities of this type of marriage and interpersonal dynamics in general with a greater sense of compassion and insight.

This understanding is crucial as we consider the teachings of Proverbs 18:21.

Life and Death: The Transformative Power of Words

Proverbs 18:21, the biblical saying, 'Death and life are in the power of the tongue, and those who love it will eat its fruits,' reminds us of the significant impact our words can have.

This wisdom teaches us that words have the power to create or destroy. 'Life' refers to positive and uplifting speech that can build and heal, while 'death' represents the potential for negative words to tear down and cause harm. This applies to everyone, regardless of their faith or beliefs.

The key message of this verse centers on the concept of 'eating' - that is, absorbing and believing - the words spoken by others or ourselves. Words' impact has no power over us until we eat and internalize them. When we accept these words, they gain the power to shape our lives in either positive or negative ways. Positive, encouraging words can lead to beneficial outcomes, whereas harmful words can result in adverse effects.

This act of internalization is akin to choosing between life and death through the words we believe.

Consider the story of Susan. When her husband, James, threatened divorce unless she lost weight, his cruel words cut to the core. Tying Susan's self-worth directly to her appearance, his ultimatum left her feeling profoundly unloved and unworthy. Struggling to cope with the emotional weight of his judgment, Susan experienced a severe breakdown.

Despite attempts to seek help, the deep scars from his words lingered, undermining her self-esteem and isolating her from potential support. Over time, the pain and isolation became too much, leaving Susan withdrawn and shadowed by a sadness that she couldn't escape.

Had Susan not internalized James's words and known her worth, his comments would have lost their sting. Knowing her worth would have turned a potential breakdown into a breakthrough, reinforcing her independence and strength. Yet, reflecting on my journey, I once was Susan. I recall CW's comment about my makeup: "He could tell when my makeup was wearing off."

This observation rattled my self-image as I took him to say my appearance without makeup was unattractive. By replaying his comments, I was eating the fruit of his word, giving him power over me, allowing his perception to dim the radiance of my self-worth. You may ask, how do you not consume negative words when you feel like what someone says is true when you struggle when complimented, or when you think they were just being polite?

This dissonance, stemming from low self-esteem, reveals the challenge of aligning internal beliefs with external feedback. For me, Jesus became my counselor and therapist as I explored the root causes of my low self-esteem; I discovered it was irreverent where it came from because Jesus's anointing had healed me from my past issues if I believed He had.

I had to internalize His words in my spirit and soul, believing in His declarations about me: I am a new creation (2 Corinthians 5:17), fearfully and wonderfully made (Psalm 139:14), God's handiwork (Ephesians 2:10), and loved with everlasting love (Jeremiah 31:3).

By actively choosing to internalize Christ's words over my and others' words, I dismantled the negative words that sought to dominate my heart. This act of faith and trust in whom God says I am empowered my capacity to decide which words shape my life. This mindset fosters a nurturing environment for inner peace, allowing me to accept myself just as God says I am.

In conclusion, it's not the words we speak that shape our destiny; the words we internalize truly determine it.

Boundaries: Lines of Love

A boundary in marriage is more than just a rule or limit. It's a mutual agreement, a shared understanding that protects our autonomy and respects each other's needs. These emotional, physical, or practical boundaries are the pillars of a healthy and balanced relationship, fostering mutual understanding and respect.

I learned about boundaries after a conversation with my daughter, Synovia. She revealed that I had crossed a boundary by sharing marital issues with her, highlighting that she didn't like it and that it was crossing a boundary she had set for our relationship. The emotional impact of this realization was profound. Crossing boundaries can lead to misunderstandings, hurt feelings, and a breakdown in trust, which can be detrimental to any relationship. After I learned about boundaries, I realized I had unintentionally crossed one with CW late one night. He didn't verbalize it, but his reaction signaled that I had crossed a boundary.

I entered his room to ask why he left the unwashed dishes. His response was startlingly out of character, and frankly, it frightened me. The following day, I brought up how his reaction had unnerved me. He confessed that he felt I was taking him for granted. I assured him that wasn't my intention and explained that his assumption was mistaken.

Moving forward, we agreed to be more open about our feelings and promptly address any perceived slights or misunderstandings. We both recognized that we had inadvertently crossed each other's boundaries without realizing it.

This conversation began a new phase in our relationship, where we strive to be more mindful of each other's boundaries. However, since CW tends to keep things to himself, we grew little from it. Nevertheless, we never crossed those boundaries again. Setting boundaries is not just about self-preservation but also about nurturing healthier interactions.

Boundaries have profoundly impacted my relationships, teaching me the importance of clear limits for mutual respect and understanding. This mutual respect is the key to maintaining peace in my marriage.

This journey underscored the adage, 'Givers must set limits because takers don't have any,' reminding me of the balance between giving to others and caring for my well-being.

What strategies can ensure boundaries are not crossed in your unequally yoked marriage?

The Art of Constructive Venting

Venting has often been painted negatively, but it's a necessary release for me. It's a way to ensure my spiritual well-being isn't compromised by bitterness, resentment, or anger.

Venting, done right, feels like shedding a heavy burden, making room for love to flow freely. This form of communication, when practiced constructively, can be a powerful tool for emotional and spiritual well-being, and I encourage you to explore its benefits. There is a thin line between venting and complaining that often gets blurred. Before I knew the difference, my behavior was akin to the constant drip on a dreary day, a symbolic reference to the 'quarrelsome wife' in Proverbs 27:15-16.

This proverb from the Old Testament is often interpreted as a warning against nagging or constant complaining, which can destroy a relationship. I recognized the power of my complaints and the need for a more constructive approach.

I began recording our discussions to address CW and my communication breakdowns. The fact that we often remembered our conversations differently led to further misunderstandings. These recordings were not made secretly but used to pinpoint and clarify misconceptions. Despite my intentions, this tactic backfired, escalating mistrust and widening our emotional gap.

CW saw it as an invasion, fearing I'd use the recordings against him. What was designed to shed light on our issues instead deepened our rift, prompting me to reflect on the unintended consequences of my approach. Differentiating between venting and complaining was crucial for transforming my approach to communication within my marriage.

I now emphasize the importance of constructive over destructive expressions of emotions. Venting is aimed at emotional release and understanding, which is beneficial with empathetic listening. Complaining focuses on expressing dissatisfaction and can strain relationships. Key differences include:

- The goal (release vs. fault-finding).
- Impact on relationships (strengthening vs. straining).
- Outcomes (healing vs. negativity).

Recognizing these distinctions aids in healthier communication and emotional well-being.

This realization hit hard. My approach needed to change. I began strategizing before approaching CW, considering potential responses and adjusting my approach accordingly. This involved thinking about what I wanted to achieve from the conversation, expressing my feelings without blaming or criticizing, and creating a safe and respectful space to share our thoughts.

I chose moments for discussion carefully, asking if this was an excellent time to talk. I initiated conversations with "I feel" statements rather than accusatory "You" statements.

Limiting my venting to release my emotions to ten minutes or less and refraining from repeating myself helped me not be wordy.

Despite my efforts to be heard, I had to acknowledge that reaching CW's heart with my words wasn't always possible. Communicating with CW was like trying to clap with one hand. His perception of my venting as complaining persisted despite my attempts to refine my approach.

However, through this process, I've discovered the power of self-reflection and self-awareness in managing my emotions and relationships. You can also harness this power to improve your communication and emotional well-being.

This journey taught me several invaluable lessons about releasing through venting and communication:

- **Stop Talking When People Stop Listening**: Recognize when your words no longer reach the listener and gracefully exit the conversation.
- **Discipline Your Disappointments**: Manage your expectations and reactions to avoid unnecessary emotional turmoil.
- **Letting Go of the Last Word**: You don't have to have the last word. Understand that winning an argument doesn't equate to resolving it.
- **Halting Conversations at the Sign of Anger**: Recognize when emotions, especially anger, begin to take over you; you should pause the discussion to prevent escalation.
- **Understand the Purpose of Venting**: Venting is a healthy emotional release when done constructively.
- **Practice Mindful Communication**: Shifting from "YOU" statements to "I" statements to express feelings without placing blame.
- **Seek Constructive Outcomes**: Focusing on resolving conflicts rather than winning arguments, fostering a more supportive and understanding relationship.

Venting is still my release, but now it's more measured and mindful. It's transformed from an emotional outpour to a concise statement, reflecting my growth in handling disappointments and communication challenges.

This evolution in how I vent has been crucial for maintaining my spiritual and emotional health, even in the face of communication barriers with CW.

Venting underscores the importance of constructively expressing oneself and knowing when to step back for personal peace and relational harmony.

How can you distinguish between constructive venting and destructive complaining to improve communication and emotional well-being in your relationships?

FORGIVENESS

My journey of forgiveness, a path strewn with personal struggles and hard-won triumphs, has been a transformative force in my life. I remember a specific incident when I could forgive a close friend who had deeply hurt me. It was a liberation from the chains of resentment and past hurts, a pathway to healing that I'm eager to share with you.

This intensely personal yet profoundly spiritual journey of forgiveness is a testament to God's power of grace and the power within us to find peace and healing by letting go. Letting go is not about forgetting or dismissing the hurt but removing its grip on you so you can live an abundant life in the present. It's a process that can bring relief and hope as you begin to see the possibilities of a life free from the burdens of the past. You have the strength within you to overcome, and God's grace is there to guide you.

I've come to see forgiveness as a divine gift, akin to the olive branch extended by God through Christ's ultimate sacrifice, as described in Ephesians 4:32. This verse encourages us to be kind and compassionate to one another and to forgive each other, just as God forgave us in Christ. This understanding wasn't immediate, especially when hurt kept popping up; it felt like a heavyweight dragging me down, making it difficult to move forward. These recurring feelings of anger, sadness, and confusion were frustrating and disheartening until I stopped trying to heal myself.

I allowed Jesus to be my therapist, counselor, and healer. How? By faith? I stood on Jesus's word.

He says the Spirit of the Lord *is* upon me because he hath anointed me to heal the brokenhearted, to preach deliverance to the captives, ...to set at liberty them that are bruised...

Luke 4:18 means that by trusting in Jesus and his teachings, I could find the strength and guidance I needed to forgive.

I learned to stand on God's Word and obey the Holy Spirit when He counseled me through God's Word. I had to choose between letting the perpetrator's actions bind me or letting Jesus's anointing heal me.

When I cried out to Jesus about the person, He instructed me to verbally affirm 'FORGIVEN' to counteract the thoughts that resurrected the painful memory of the perpetrator's actions.

I spoke God's word over my hurt. I blessed the perpetrator. (Matthew 5:44) My practice of forgiveness was a steady, intentional effort.

By continuously uttering the word 'forgiven,' I drew power from the Holy Spirit within me, standing and feeding off God's strength to empower me to forgive. (Matthew 6:14-16) It became a frequent occurrence for me to repeat the word 'FORGIVE' multiple times throughout the day whenever these distressing thoughts attempted to invade my mind.

This process of active affirmation and drawing strength from God's grace was crucial in my journey of forgiveness.

Thus, true forgiveness is a holistic endeavor. It's not just about forgiving the person who hurt us but also about forgiving ourselves for holding onto the hurt, healing the emotional wounds, and understanding the lessons learned from the experience.

It requires aligning the spirit with divine teachings, soothing the soul's wounds, and caring for the body that manifests our wounded emotions.

To forgive fully, we must attend to each part of ourselves, understanding how these elements interconnect and influence our ability to let go and move forward.

Forgiveness, a testament to your faith in God's healing power, is not a sign of weakness but a profound strength. To navigate the tumultuous journey of forgiveness, you must rely on your faith in God's ability to heal you.

First, acknowledge and accept the feelings of anger, betrayal, or pain caused by another's actions. Denying these emotions can hinder your healing. If applicable, communicate your feelings to the person who wronged you, as expressing your hurt can be a critical part of moving forward.

Next, make a conscious decision to forgive. Remember, forgiveness is a choice you make not because the other person necessarily deserves it but because you deserve peace.

Let go of any grudges and bitterness to allow yourself emotional freedom. Trust in this process, and you will find the peace you seek.

It's crucial to set realistic expectations. Don't expect an apology or a change in the person you are forgiving; forgiveness is a personal journey, not a tool for altering others. Instead, focus on your healing and growth and trust that forgiveness will lead you to peace and freedom.

Lastly, shift your focus from the past to the future. Embrace new opportunities and experiences that promote your well-being and happiness. This is where the anointing of Jesus comes into play. His anointing equips you with the strength and direction to progress, embrace fresh starts, and discover joy and fulfillment in your life.

These are the tools for managing relationships and the essential components of forgiveness. We nurture resilience, stimulate personal growth, and foster emotional maturity by adopting these practices and forgiveness. These steps assist us in managing our relationships more effectively and empower us to lead more prosperous, more fulfilling lives.

Jesus deals with each one of us differently. If you feel you need professional help, get it. Just remember that true healing comes from Jesus Christ.

Are there any barriers or emotions that currently make it difficult for you to forgive, and how might turning to God's word help you overcome these obstacles?

CHAPTER 18

Sanctuary of the Soul

Prayer

Prayer is what keeps our spiritual life alive. It is our protective enclave, shielding our hearts and minds from the anxieties of life. It is more than a spiritual duty; it is the breath of life, a sacred conversation with God that transcends earthly confinement.

Prayer has been my refuge and strength, helping me navigate the often-challenging dynamics of an unequally yoked marriage and life. It allows me to find balance in my confusion. In a world fraught with chaos and uncertainty, prayer offers a unique peace that transcends earthly troubles.

As I turn my thoughts away from the noise and demands of daily life, I find in prayer a quiet place where I can reconnect with my inner self and God.

This peace is reflected in Philippians 4:6-7, which encourages, "Do not be anxious about anything, but in every situation, by prayer and petition, with thanksgiving, present your requests to God. And the peace of God, which transcends all understanding, will guard your hearts and minds in Christ Jesus."

Prayer is my bridge of faith to get God's promises. With each uttered plea and silent confession, I engage in a transformational exchange, laying bare my deepest fears and loftiest dreams.

This act transcends mere supplication; it is an offering of my most authentic self, reminiscent of Psalm 51:17, "The sacrifices of God are a broken spirit: a broken and a contrite heart, O God, thou wilt not despise."

This profound interaction molds my spirit, strengthens my resolve, and imbues peace within my restless soul. Prayer deepens my relationship with God, turning my dialogues into lifelines that anchor me.

Scriptures like 1 John 5:14-15, "And this is the confidence that we have in him, that, if we ask anything according to his will, he heareth us: And if we know that he hears us, whatsoever we ask, we know that we have the petitions that we desired of him."

This scripture bolsters my confidence, assuring me that God hears and answers my prayers. It strengthens me to be a supportive wife while staying true to my faith. The essence of prayer lies not in altering God's grand design but in transforming me, aligning my soul with His divine will, and granting clarity and serenity as I rise, renewed.

In prayer, I find the assurance of 2 Corinthians 12:9, "My grace is sufficient for you, for my power is made perfect in weakness." In this light, prayer is akin to a golden scepter, empowering me to approach God's throne boldly, where I find mercy and grace in times of need.

This empowerment was evident when I faced a critical decision to love my spouse when it wasn't reciprocated, which conflicted with my flesh. Prayer brought clarity and peace, affirming God's will to teach me to love aligned with God's larger plan for my life.

In moments of pain and loss, especially when feeling isolated in my spiritual practices, what some might call 'divine silence' has been a teacher. These periods echo the experiences of biblical figures like Job and the Apostle Paul, who found strength in their faith despite God's silence.

As James 5:16 declares, "The effectual fervent prayer of a righteous man availeth much."

Through prayer, realities shift, internal and external; We emerge as one knowing something new about God that we didn't know before. These silent moments are filled with God's subtle work. They teach me patience, nurture my faith, and provide a comforting anchor in life's storms.

Scriptures like Hebrews 13:5, "I will never leave you nor forsake you," are not just words but a deep, enduring assurance.

This promise has been incredibly comforting during nights when the solitude of my spiritual path could have been overwhelming. Yet, I felt God's quiet, steadfast presence providing hope and encouragement.

What is the significance of divine silence in prayer, and how can it deepen faith?

Worship

Worship is my spiritual booster. It's a sanctuary for my spirit, offering a profound spiritual refuge where I need to connect with God and find renewal. Through worship, I experience a profound, personal bond that brings me peace and deepens and transforms my inner man.

Singing worship songs transcends routine; it rejuvenates my soul, clears my mind, and strengthens my faith. This form of worship is a vibrant spiritual practice that acts as a booster, elevating me above the everyday worries of life.

However, there have been times when it felt like God wasn't inhabiting my worship. During these moments, the divine presence I so deeply relied on seemed distant, leaving me singing into what felt like an empty void. In these times of spiritual silence, I have paused to examine my life for any sins or barriers hindering my connection with God.

If I found none, I would persevere, continuing to worship with the faith that He was there even though His presence wasn't palpable.

God promises in Hebrews 13:5 that He will never leave or forsake us, a truth I cling to, especially when the emotional experience of worship doesn't align with my expectations.

I recall a particularly challenging time when I was anxious and uncertain about the future. I had gotten fired for missing too many days due to my pregnancy; with no savings at six months pregnant and CW just starting a new job, the world seemed heavy and bleak. Amid this profound agony, when words failed me, and I struggled to articulate my pain, worship through music became my voice. Each lyric took my worries and fears as I gave tribute to my God's sovereignty and holiness. Worship provided a powerful medium to express my faith in His provisions.

By the song's end, my mood had transformed, and I felt recharged with spiritual energy, ready to face my challenges with renewed faith and courage. God had inhabited my worship. This experience underscores how worship can significantly boost the spirit, grounding one in peace and equipping one with resilience.

This practice is a steadfast part of my life. I worship God for who He is, not only in times of distress but also in my abundance. Worshiping and praising God transforms my perspective, renewing my spirit. It fortifies my heart and refreshes my mind, allowing me to face the world's chaos with renewed strength.

Moreover, worship has taught me that God is truly in control, a realization that has been instrumental in maintaining my positive outlook and resilience in the face of adversity. It inspires me to keep moving forward with gratitude.

In worship, I have found a sanctuary where my spirit can survive and thrive, drawing from an inexhaustible well of divine strength. Worship is more than a practice—it is a lifeline we can embrace to find solace and strength in times of despair.

Through worship, we learn that even in our lowest moments, we can raise our voices in song and connect with the divine God, finding peace and purpose amidst the trials.

Prayer and worship are vital practices and transformative experiences that nurture our spiritual life. They are the sanctuaries where we encounter God's sufficiency and mercy, our weaknesses are met with His strength, and His steadfast presence envelops our solitude.

As we continue on our spiritual journeys, may we consistently find solace and strength in these divine sanctuaries, ever-growing in our faith and love of God.

Let us cherish these sacred prayer and worship spaces, for our souls and spirits find true sanctuary and are continually transformed.

How can worship through music transform your deepest struggles into powerful testimonies of faith and resilience?

CHAPTER 19

The Pursuit of Lost Connection

CW and I's marriage was a fusion of two souls, each carrying its unique history and emotional baggage. I, with my blend of insecurities, a deep yearning for love, anger, and a tendency towards codependency. These were the echoes of my past, silently shaping the narrative of our relationship. On his part, CW bore the scars of his upbringing and a previous marriage tainted by distrust.

My blend of insecurities, anger, and codependency fostered a situation where CW's efforts never seemed adequate, transforming my continual pleas into what felt like relentless criticism and my persistent insecurities about his love into rapid anger when needs were unfulfilled.

This constant need for validation and my habit of challenging everything he expressed became overwhelming, inadvertently pushing him to shut down emotionally and harboring bitterness in his heart.

The pain of unrequited love, of feeling like my needs were never met, was a constant companion. In hindsight, I see how my actions, driven by my fears and dependencies, contributed significantly to the strain on our relationship.

My inability to recognize and manage my emotions effectively hindered our communication and placed an unfair burden on CW, making it difficult for him to meet my ever-shifting expectations.

As the eldest child of a single mother with eight boys, CW learned to see requests as burdensome commands, and his previous marriage was plagued by suspicion. Every time I asked for his help, my request inadvertently triggered a maternal demand in his mind, driving him further into isolation. He felt like a bobblehead, mechanically nodding to my pleas, a metaphor for his compliance. This perspective became his truth, A lens through which he viewed our interactions.

Even my gentlest requests seemed to stir memories, adding layers to our complex dynamic. His increasing distance was a defense against perceived losses of autonomy.

Shadows of his former marriage linger in ours, tainting our moments with doubt and mistrust.

Despite my sincere efforts, he viewed my actions through a lens clouded by past scars, haunted by specters he could not seem to escape. This scrutiny has eroded his trust, making fostering intimacy and understanding challenging.

I have passionately implored him to see me as I am — distinct from the echoes of his previous struggles.

Our shared history has led to a mutual struggle in our attempts to connect, even in the most ordinary situations.

The barrier that has grown between us is not just a product of our different ways of dealing with emotions but also a result of unresolved conflict.

It's not about specific wrongdoings but about the fact that we were not truly listening, not hearing each other.

We both have our ways of dealing with emotions. He keeps his feelings locked away while I am more open. This has led to a mutual disconnect, as if the other doesn't care. This emotional distance is not just a burden for one of us but for both. As a result, this cycle has contributed to my pursuit and CW's emotional retreat, further deepening the emotional rifts in our marriage.

At this juncture, it became evident that our combined baggage heavily and our spiritual mismatch influenced our marriage dynamics. Reflecting on these, I recognize how these dynamics strained our relationship, leading to moments where we both felt misunderstood and distant.

Recognizing my role in our patterns, I sought Jesus' healing touch to mend my troubles, fill the voids in my soul, and heal my emotional scars. CW did not seek healing or turn to Jesus for the restoration he needed, resulting in ongoing issues in our relationship.

As he remained anchored in his past wounds, this divergence in our approaches to healing led to his minimal constructive contribution to our marriage, further widening the gap between us.

Diminishing Intimacy:

In the seventeenth year of our marriage, CW's behavior significantly changed. The harshness and condescension that had once defined his interactions with me decreased. I believe this change resulted from a moment when, after one of his critical outbursts, I reminded him that we would have to answer to God for how we spoke to each other.

CW chose silence over dialogue in response, resorting to the silent treatment. This new depth of silence proved more challenging than his previous critical words; the absence of communication was, in its way, more painful.

At least before, I had some insight into his thoughts and feelings. Now, I was left to navigate the void of his unspoken words, a silence that spoke volumes yet revealed little.

CW and I were lying in bed one evening, engrossed in a deep conversation about life. Unexpectedly, a misunderstanding arose, and I said something that upset him. The exact words that sparked the discord are lost. Neither of us remembers what was said, but whatever was said didn't warrant his departure.

During our conversation, he abruptly got up and left the room. That night marked the last time CW would share our bed, leaving behind a void that was filled with confusion and heartache.

The reason for CW's sudden departure from our shared space remained a mystery. When asked why he left our bedroom, he attributed his concern for my sleep to coming to bed late and not wanting to disturb me because I got up early to work—a reason that both of us knew was not the truth. This incident taught me a valuable lesson—the bedroom should be a sanctuary of romance, where disagreements are left at the door, no matter how trivial.

His physical exit from our bedroom deepened his emotional departure from our marriage. His yearning remained evidenced by his physical advances.

However, even that dwindled as the days turned to months and months to years. This emotional weight bore down on me. I hid his departure from our bedroom, the weight only lifting years later when I confided in my sister.

According to research, a considerable portion of married couples experience separate sleeping arrangements or dwindling intimacy. The root causes often are deeper emotional disconnections or sexual dissatisfaction.

As time went on, his withdrawal persisted; he even stopped washing his clothes with mine. The little acts of love I cherished doing for him- cooking his favorite meals, preparing his coffee, little gestures of care - he no longer wanted me to do.

My attempts to give him something special because I loved him, he didn't open them.

Our intimacy also suffered; he stopped initiating intimacy with me but accepted my advances, but the affection, kissing, hugging, and warmth that once accompanied them were conspicuously absent.

If I didn't initiate our intimacy and conversation or go where he was in our home, he would be content to live as if he were single.

A pivotal moment of clarity came when I began to view our marriage through CW's lens. My observations over the years slowly illuminated how my challenges to his viewpoints, advice-giving, and criticisms of his wisdom, especially in front of our children, contributed to his growing bitterness. This journey of self-discovery and understanding my role in our relationship was an eye-opener.

For instance, when he advised our children that changing people, places, and things was essential to stay out of trouble, I would inadvertently counter his point and say that internal change was more critical; external changes were futile without removing the foolishness in one's heart.

Also, CW seemed to dismiss our sons' promiscuous behavior as typical boyhood antics, but I opposed this view, citing God's teachings about sexuality. However, this approach appeared to him as a criticism of his wisdom. It made him feel undermined as a man and contributed to his growing bitterness toward me.

Note: When your spouse, who may not share your beliefs, offers advice to the children or makes a statement you disagree with, refrain from openly challenging them in the presence of the kids.

My Efforts to Reconnect

To be a better spouse, I embarked on various strategies: proposing marriage counseling, engaging in marriage-related activities like listening to CDs, monthly relationship check-ins, and even role-playing. CW's willingness to participate gave me hope, but his involvement remained minimal, and he struggled to apply what we had learned. My efforts to salvage our marriage seemed to frustrate him, and he often felt like a bobblehead, nodding along without fully engaging.

As my faith deepened, I witnessed a transformation in myself over the years. I became more patient, less reactive, and keen to mend bridges. I love CW; however, CW seemed to drift further away as I applied Christ's characteristics to my life. His consistent allegations—that I always had an attitude and believed I knew everything, always wanted to be correct, or somehow considered myself superior to others—bewildered me.

I encouraged him to highlight moments when I might come off as a "know-it-all" so I could understand where he was coming from.

Recognizing my journey and its inevitable flaws, I often apologized to CW, even when the accusations against me were unfounded. I did this in pursuit of peace.

During my prayer, I said, "Lord, I am earnestly striving to live by Your Word within my marriage. Yet, I am also humbly seeking clarity about CW's perceptions of me. If there is any truth in his words, I ask You to reveal it to me."

As I continued to pray, a profound sense of peace washed over me, affirming that my actions aligned with His will. It became apparent that CW's perception was of the old me, a version I had long left behind. This realization revealed that CW and I were experiencing our relationship through different realities, with CW navigating his distinct perspective.

Seeking More Understanding

I approached CW, asking for forgiveness for any perceived wrongs, and pleaded with him to release any pent-up resentment he harbored against me. My efforts at love couldn't unclog the bitterness he felt towards me.

Throughout our marriage, I consistently made it clear to CW that I was committed for life, bound by the vow of 'till death do us part' regardless of my happiness unless he broke our bond through infidelity or desertion. Nevertheless, I also stressed that if he was unwilling to invest in our marriage or didn't want me, he should set me free, or better yet, free himself.

Divine Guidance

I brought my frustration to God, questioning why my attempts at love seemed to backfire. "I'm trying to be the wife You desire me to be, but loving CW is like hugging a fan; I get sliced up in the process. Confused by my sowing love's inability to reciprocate CW's love confused me, I turned to God to remind Him of Galatians 6:7-9.

"Do not be deceived: God cannot be mocked. A man reaps what he sows. Whoever sows to please their flesh, from the flesh, will reap destruction; whoever sows to please the Spirit, from the Spirit, will reap eternal life."

Lord, am I not sowing and showing love in my marriage? That's when I had a divine inclination to read John 3:16,

"For God so loved the world, that he gave his only begotten Son, that whosoever believeth in him should not perish but have everlasting life. "

Upon first and even second reading of John 3:16, I couldn't see why the Spirit prompted me to read the verse. However, in the third reading of John 3:16, several keywords stood out:

- **God loved**
- **He gave**
- **Whosoever believes**

The Spirit highlighted God's love for humanity that He gave His Son. However, only whosoever believes or accepts His ever-present love will foster a reciprocal relationship when it is actively received. Absent this reception, God's constant love remains ineffectual in altering a person's heart to love Him back.

The Spirit's message revealed that love is akin to a gift that, although given freely, only holds value and brings joy when the intended recipient accepts and cherishes it. In CW's case, his inability to return my love directly resulted from his choice not to take the love I offered, thus foreclosing the possibility of a loving exchange between us.

This revelation reminded me of a past prayer when God restored me, during which I sought His guidance to learn to love as He taught the Thessalonians. This profound revelation, which emerged through CW's rejection and lack of desire for me, was God's conduit to teach me how to love.

This influential instructor revealed the depths and challenges of striving to love in the manner of God's unconditional love. Unrequited love is a painful, one-sided affair filled with grief, shame, and the torment of seeking fulfillment from an empty vessel.

By Practicing Love, I Learn to Love

God still required me to love CW in the shadow of the Spirit's revelation about why my love wasn't changing CW. This revelation filled my heart with understanding a lesson in practicing love under the most trying circumstances.

Paul's teachings about whatever you do, do it as unto the Lord and not to man became my critical guidepost. Viewing my actions towards CW as if done unto Jesus proved more challenging than I initially anticipated. I sought solace in Jesus, feeling disheartened after attempting to show CW kindness or when I went to his room looking for connection, like watching TV together. I yearn for the affectionate embrace we once shared, but it remained elusive. Each time, I tried to hug him. I was met with indifference; every attempt to share a kiss was left without passion.

In this cycle of seeking and not finding, I often pondered the nature of my persistence. Lord, are You urging me to continue offering love unconditionally, or was it merely the inherent yearning of my heart?

This question became a recurring theme in my reflections, a whisper in the quiet moments of disappointment.

Upon expressing my frustrations to Jesus, an unexpected insight emerged. Jesus, **in His infinite wisdom,** clarified that feelings of anger, frustration, humiliation, or the impulse to complain indicated that my actions were self-serving rather than dedicated to Him.

This realization struck me: when one genuinely acts to do it unto Jesus, such negative emotions and complaints will dissipate once realized they are done unto the Lord, for the work is done in honor of Him.

Therefore, any anger or dissatisfaction following what I believed Jesus was instructing me to do, even when it was rejected or the good deed done wasn't appreciated, highlighted a heart preoccupied with its interests, not entirely doing the deed as unto Jesus.

This revelation made it more accessible to perform and helped me understand the true motivations behind my actions.

However, throughout these challenging years, I remained steadfast in my commitment to our marriage.

Despite the humiliation and heartache, I continued to love CW, and whatever I did unto him, I dedicated it to the Lord. I got to a point where CW's rejection didn't fade me. I had conquered it through love for God.

CW, are you content with how things are?" I ventured, hoping for a glimpse into his feelings. "I'm good," he would invariably respond, a veil of simplicity over the depth of his thoughts.

Doubts crept in, leading me to inquire cautiously about another person's existence in his life. He dismissed the idea outright.

"Why do you seem so distant towards me?" I asked, seeking some understanding. His silence was the only answer I received, teaching me a harsh lesson about our communication and the depth of the divide between us. This silence, louder than any words, underscored a growing distance I had yet to comprehend fully.

I was bewildered; CW's persistent suspicion thwarted my efforts to express love, reflecting the strained relationship between Saul and David. No matter how earnestly David showed loyalty and affection, Saul harbored unyielding bitterness towards him.

Yet, I continued to reach out, but I quickly said, 'If you don't want to work on the marriage, or you don't want me, then set me free, set yourself free. Why do you stay in the marriage if you're not happy? His response was, "Why do you stay?"

Rooted in my vows to God and drawing my happiness from Him, I respond, even when love seems absent in our marriage.

Years passed with this repetitive cycle until I acknowledged the truth: he didn't want a connection with me. Our dynamic resembled the age-old chase—me pursuing and him retreating.

Our disconnect wasn't just due to our different spiritual natures, or his emotional withdrawal, or my heightened emotions; it was the combination.

I couldn't see it then, but this enduring quest for affection was shaping me in ways I had not anticipated. What felt like a relentless pursuit of CW's warmth was, in truth, a lesson in unconditional love, to give without awaiting return, much like how God taught the Thessalonians to love as a testament to their faith and resilience.

This journey was a complex, often painful teaching, but in the end, I learned the true essence of happiness and love—a patient, kind, and selfless love that echoes God's teachings, urging us to love as we are loved.

As you navigate your life's journey, ask yourself: Whom is God using to teach you how to love?

CHAPTER 20:

The Gradual Disintegration

Echoes of Neglect

On a sunny Saturday morning, I looked out the back window. CW was standing by the road, his eyes scanning the street. I thought little of it until an unfamiliar SUV pulled up beside him. Watching quietly, I saw my husband lean down with a smile to peer into the vehicle. His body obscured my view of the driver, but I noticed a woman inside as he pointed her to pull up and park.

I retreated from the kitchen, unwilling to be seen by him in my curious state. I watched from another room; my view was limited to him alone. His demeanor was remarkably enthusiastic, displaying a side of him I hadn't witnessed for decades. He was bubbly and animated in conversation with this unknown woman, a stark contrast to the sternness he showed me.

I wondered who this woman was who had rekindled such liveliness in my husband. Their ease of conversation suggested familiarity. I couldn't hear them, but CW's laughter and free-flowing talk were unmistakable.

He reached into the vehicle at one point – did he touch her? I felt a sinking in my heart as I realized she was receiving the emotional connection I had longed for from him. For forty-seven minutes, I witnessed my husband reveal a part of himself that he had ceased sharing with me.

After they parted, I confronted him about this interaction and approached him to discuss what had transpired. I expressed my feelings openly, saying, 'Husband, I noticed that you provided that woman with something I've been longing for from you for years.

It seemed so effortless for you to offer it to her. Can you explain why that is? He explained she was Laurel from the Boulevard projects and wanted a follow-up interview, yet he didn't answer my question.

His justification did not ease my overwhelming feelings of neglect, and the ease with which he connected with her reignited my longstanding feelings of being unloved and undervalued in our marriage.

He had previously informed me about his interview, which was broadcast on television, so I knew he was telling the truth. Yet, understanding the context didn't ease my emotional turmoil. I came to accept the truth; my place in his heart was gone.

Liberation Through Faith

Remarkably, this scene didn't bring me despair but a profound sense of empowerment. The intricate knots that had once tightly bound me to CW, which I thought were impossible to untangle, had dissipated. My spiritual growth through the years gradually strengthened me to utilize Christ's authority to unravel these once seemingly unbreakable ties.

Choosing to be proactive instead of reactive, I took control of my emotions and directed my responses rather than allowing them to lead me toward negativity. This deliberate shift in my approach marked a significant victory over the adverse effects of disappointment.

As I pondered how easily CW communicated with Laurel, I realized I had committed relational suicide throughout our marriage, assuming I could win him over by argument, sweet reasonableness, or any other common wisdom.

Even Christian virtues like love, gentleness, patience, and turning the other cheek only deepened my efforts. To relate to CW takes uncommon wisdom that can be gleaned only by those who genuinely desire it. I refer to that wisdom as "relational intelligence." Why not test your relational intelligence by taking this brief quiz? Answer 'yes' or 'no' to the questions, and then we'll look at what your answers tell us about your relationship dynamics.

RELATIONAL INTELLIGENCE

This assessment aims to evaluate rational thinking within an unequally yoked marriage. The following questions are designed to help identify areas of potential concern and promote a healthier understanding of marital dynamics.

Yes No

☐ ☐ Do you often feel self-pity when your spouse rejects your efforts or advances?

☐ ☐ Has anyone ever mentioned that you act differently when your spouse is around?

☐ ☐ Do you always try to calm your spouse when they are angry, regardless of the situation?

☐ ☐ Do you ever think this isn't so bad?

☐ ☐ Do you rationalize your spouse's irrational or hurtful behavior to yourself or others?

☐ ☐ Do you believe that improving your appearance could make your partner more interested in you?

☐ ☐ Do your spouse's opinions and judgments influence your perception of yourself?

☐ ☐ Do you often change your behavior to seek approval from your spouse?

☐ ☐ Do you think conforming more to your spouse's demands would improve your marriage?

☐ ☐ Are you of the opinion that your actions are the main reason for your spouse's anger?

☐ ☐ Do you feel you can't be true to yourself around your unbeliever?

☐ ☐ Do you feel that your spouse is often dissatisfied with you?

☐ ☐ Do you frequently feel responsible for your spouse's well-being?

☐ ☐ Do you blame yourself for your spouse emotionally distancing themselves from the relationship?

If your response is 'yes' to five or more questions, it may indicate that you struggle significantly with your unbelieving spouse as I did. This struggle often manifests as emotional turmoil, trapping you in repetitive cycles and unresolved conflicts that can persist for years.

In such marriages, it is crucial to enhance your relational intelligence—the ability to understand and manage your relationships effectively. Simple, conventional wisdom may not be sufficient; instead, you must seek the wisdom that comes from God, as advised in James 3:13-18.

Believing that demonstrating virtues like love, gentleness, patience, or kindness in adversity will automatically change your unbelieving spouse is a misconception. Love is not always reciprocated, especially in a marriage with differing spiritual natures. In such situations, it is crucial to prioritize God's love for you and your own mental and emotional well-being.

Believing that you can change your unbelieving spouse through arguments, a gentle approach, or other common tactics is often misguided. What's required is a deep understanding and application of divine wisdom, seeking guidance from God, and applying His teachings in your marriage.

It's essential to recognize that being guided by the Holy Spirit doesn't eliminate challenges. Anticipating that your non-believing spouse will cause spiritual and emotional distress is not a misjudgment.

As I continued to grow in Christ, I endeavored to emulate Jesus' teachings, hoping that my demonstration of love and compassion would eventually lead to CW's understanding and acceptance of the transformed me.

Yet, despite my prayers and efforts, the acceptance I longed for has yet to materialize. It seemed like CW wanted to be free from our marriage but was held back by something.

In our marriage, being near CW often left me feeling constrained. Whenever I saw things differently and expressed my opinions, like political views and life itself, CW took my point of view as a sign that I believed I was always correct, knew it all, sought to have things my way, or felt superior to others. Yet, our marriage held us together for personal and varied reasons. My commitment to our union was, first and foremost, a vow before God — a promise I intended to keep until death do us part or unless CW renounced our sacred bond himself.

God chose CW for his kindness yet firm heart, a provider who, despite his strengths, could not grasp the nuances of intimacy a wife craves. In CW, I saw what could be considered the pinnacle of partners among nonbelievers.

CW is decent, neither abusive nor a man given to derogatory remarks or base indulgences. He was a provider who chose the warmth of home over the streets and the world's temptations. Every gesture of kindness from CW throughout our marriage, no matter how small, was a treasure to me, and I ensured he knew how much I appreciated his efforts. My only vice with him was that he didn't love me.

Our marriage had great potential. Yet, within this marriage that lacked the love and emotional connection I craved, I eventually found completeness and happiness in Christ Jesus—a testament to the divine grace that enabled me to stay and the faith that empowered me to finish honoring my vow to God through it all. These gifts of grace and faith instructed me to unearth joy and peace in Christ Jesus amidst so little emotional satisfaction in my marriage.

In my last attempt to connect with my husband, I invited him to watch 'Hope Springs' in our living room, hoping the movie would help him understand my feelings about our marriage.

I explained, "This movie reflects our marriage," aiming to initiate a heartfelt conversation. However, his reaction was disheartening; he arrived late and chose to sit opposite me. After the movie, I asked, "What did you think?" He silently got up and left, leaving my attempts at connection unanswered. At that moment, clarity washed over me like a cold wave breaking against the shore. The painful truth emerged from the fog of my hopes and dreams: he had no interest in preserving our marriage.

I was standing at a crossroads, realizing he no longer valued me or intended to meet the basic needs of marriage. This epiphany forced me to confront a harsh reality, signaling a pivotal shift in my perspective. It was time for me to gather my strength and wisdom. It was a moment of awakening. I asked myself, why are you trying to hold on to something that doesn't want to be held? It was a call to see myself through a lens unclouded by his indifference. I recognized the necessity of forging my path toward self-recovery, leaving behind the shadow of a relationship that had since left me.

After careful consideration of prayer, fasting, and profoundly honoring my commitment to God to respect my marriage covenant, I decided to pursue a route of inner detachment while still participating in our shared life.

CW had not violated our marriage covenant, which I knew of, and my decision to continue our shared life was grounded in profound faith and dedication to my vow to God and spiritual obligations.

Knowing the depth of love, I had to share; I concluded that staying within my marriage was more reasonable than leaving to live a life of singleness when I had so much love to give.

I cherish the concept of marriage, and I believe that had I encountered someone while single, I would have remarried and found reasons to justify my actions.

However, I did not wish to place myself in a situation that could compromise my principles or breach God's commands again. This choice of detaching internally allowed me to walk in peace, holding onto my values and the sanctity of our marriage vows.

It was a testament to my belief that honoring one's commitments, even in the face of unmet expectations. While living together, detaching from my unbelieving spouse involves a nuanced understanding and application of supernatural spiritual wisdom.

It's not just about emotional separation; it's an inner journey of faith and trust in God's plan for both individuals. This process requires patience, compassion, and discernment.

I encountered some difficulties while trying to distance myself from CW. At first, I considered emulating his behavior as a justifiable reaction. This entailed reducing our interactions to a minimum, like basic greetings, and refraining from wearing my wedding ring. I did not inform him of my whereabouts when I left our residence. I took these measures to be equitable and reciprocate CW's detachment.

Upon being guided by the Holy Spirit, I was reminded of the importance of embodying Christ's teachings as a godly wife, independently of CW's demeanor and aligning with my spiritual convictions. This prompted a conscientious effort to ensure my actions aligned with Christian values. I aimed to maintain a good conscience, living in a way that those who might speak ill of me would find themselves mistaken, witnessing a life lived by Christ's example. (1 Peter 3:16) As a result, I started wearing my wedding ring again and sharing details of my whereabouts.

I redirected my focus from seeking CW's affection to cultivating profound devotion to God and self-love. Treating CW with the same detached kindness I would extend to a stranger, paradoxically, CW seemed as if my detachment was what he wanted. This increased his engagement with me, initiating conversations and telling me where he was going when he left our home.

However, this dynamic change was brief, interrupted by different points of view that caused CW to withdraw into silence once again. I surrendered CW to God, stopped reacting to his opinions, and continued walking in the spiritual blessings that are mine in Jesus.

This strategy helped me find inner peace. I realized that my efforts to please CW were futile and that I had wasted precious time. You may question whether this way of living constitutes a marriage in the ideal sense. The answer is no. Yet, it represents a commitment to the role and responsibilities I embraced upon taking my wedding vows, and CW was willing to stay. (1 Corinthians 7:12)

God reveals Himself in remarkable ways when we choose the challenging path of obedience, honor Him, and entrust the resolution of our circumstances to His wisdom without insisting on our solutions.

How can one step back from a spouse's controlling behavior while living together as a married couple? What options are there if biblical standards don't justify divorce? Exceedingly, when your unbelieving partner hasn't been unfaithful or deserted you but instead remains as constant as ever. This predicament is common and calls for significant insight and discernment.

Thus, embrace wisdom as your most trusted ally and treat understanding like a cherished family member. (Proverbs 7:4) In doing so, you'll find the strength and guidance to navigate these complex waters, forging a path that honors your integrity and commitment to your marriage.

Scripture outlines two pathways for a Christian in a marriage with an unbeliever. The first option encourages staying in the marriage and treating the unbelieving partner with peace, quietness, and gentleness, drawing from the guidance of Romans 12:18 and 1 Peter 3:1-2.

The second path is separation, with the condition of remaining single or being open to reconciliation, as 1 Corinthians 7:10-11 suggests. This directive upholds the sanctity and commitment of marriage while recognizing the unique challenges presented by being unequally yoked.

Deciding whether to continue in peaceful coexistence or to choose separation requires thoughtful reflection, an understanding of one's faith, and consideration of personal situations.

If God has endowed you with the strength and grace to share your life with a partner marked by strife, folly, or one who does not reciprocate love, accepting this trial is part of your divine purpose while nurturing an inner peace that is grounded in your trust and hope in God.

Peace is imperative in marriage. It guides me as I persevere and reminds me that my well-being and spiritual tranquility are paramount as I navigate this challenging path of being in an unequally yoked marriage.

This path is not merely about tolerating difficult circumstances; it's an active engagement in faith, demonstrating resilience, being joyful in the joy of the Lord, and trusting in God's plan. In such situations, it's crucial to cultivate patience, understanding, and a spirit of forgiveness, recognizing these qualities as reflections of divine love.

However, establishing healthy boundaries and safeguarding your spiritual, emotional, and mental well-being are equally important. If entrusting your unbelieving spouse to God's care represents surrender, it's natural to question why letting go is challenging. This inner conflict often arises when your unbelieving spouse reacts negatively to the perceptible shift in your demeanor.

As a result, their response might manifest as anger in various forms. They might accuse you of abandonment, express discomfort with the changes in you that they find disagreeable, or even lash out, either physically, verbally, or emotionally, frustrated by your seeming failure to meet their expectations.

Alternatively, they might withdraw, using silence as a form of punishment. It's essential to recognize that your unbelieving spouse may perceive your transformation as a loss of control, which can threaten them.

This situation requires understanding and patience as you navigate this complex dynamic while staying true to your faith and personal happiness.

Understanding the Difference between Abuse and Persecution in Marriage

An abusive marriage and persecution are both forms of oppression but differ significantly in scope and nature. An abusive marriage is a personal relationship where one partner exerts control through violence, manipulation, or coercion, creating a private power imbalance that severely impacts the victim's health and stability. If you feel your life is in danger, seek help immediately.

However, persecution within a marriage, when experienced for one's beliefs rather than through abusive behavior, can be a unique trial that teaches us to seek refuge in God and grow spiritually. It deepens our dependence on Him and develops Christ's character in us. While this kind of persecution is not abusive in a conventional sense, it still poses significant emotional challenges and requires strength and faith to endure.

Understanding these distinctions ensures that support and advocacy are tailored to each form of oppression's unique challenges, allowing people to get needed help or experience spiritual growth and healing aligned with spiritual principles.

Journeying towards Detachment

Untangling yourself from your unbeliever doesn't imply that you cease to care; instead, it means you stop attempting to compel your unbeliever to care similarly. Remember, it's about balancing loving your spouse and staying true to your spiritual convictions.

The first step toward untangling yourself is purposeful prayer and fasting. Humbly approach God and admit that you require His supernatural wisdom because you are unsure what to say or do. God welcomes sincere prayers from the heart.

Secondly, let go and admit there is nothing you can do to change the heart of your unbelieving spouse; that task is reserved for God alone.

Thirdly, if God has graced you to stay with your unbelieving spouse, maintain an attitude of love. This love does not entail reciprocating their negative actions but responding with God's love.

Fourth, resist being drawn into arguments by your unbelieving spouse. Maintain your composure by focusing on the things above, and hum you a spiritual hymn. It takes two to argue; when CW would throw a bait out, I would say, "You do you. I am doing Jesus.

"The beginning of strife is like letting out water, so abandon the quarrel before it breaks out." (Proverbs 17:14 NASB95).

Fifth, combat evil with goodness, even when it initially feels awkward. As you persist, you will witness changes in your heart as you learn to act in the spirit of Christ (Romans 12:11–17).

Sixth, speak the truth in love when you find yourself angered. Avoid responding with bitterness and anger, as it can give the devil a foothold (Ephesians 4:25–27).

Remember, an insult is like mud; brushing it off when it dries is easier.

Seventh, trust God, stand firm, and draw strength from Him. The accurate measure of your faith becomes evident during turbulent times.

As I close this chapter, I leave you with this: **Martyrdom does not transform people; only God does. Let go and allow God to work. You have nothing to prove to anyone except God Himself.**

CHAPTER 21

Reshaping Bonds

In May 2023, a revelation blindsided me, casting a deep shadow over my marriage. My husband, with whom I had journeyed through life for 33 years, calmly disclosed that he had been approved for an apartment in New Orleans. The news struck me like a bolt out of the blue.

The previous year, we had taken what I thought was a leisurely vacation to New Orleans, but it now dawned on me that this trip might have been the catalyst for his secretive decision. The realization that he had been planning to leave, meticulously orchestrating his departure without my knowledge for over a year, was shocking and heart-wrenching.

It was a bitter pill to swallow, knowing that I was the last to be informed, an afterthought in a decision uprooting the foundation of our shared existence.

Almost in passing, he mentioned that he would move into his new apartment on July 7, 2023. This date, now etched in my memory, symbolized more than just a change of address; it represented the desertion of our marriage covenant. But amid this storm, I found a strength I never knew I had, a resilience that would carry me through the darkest days.

The Silent Goodbye

On July 7, 2023, CW decisively exited our marriage, a departure I had come to anticipate and longed for. While he was packing, I found myself seated on his bed, engaging in what felt like a normal conversation. Later, retreating to my room, I succumbed to a brief doze. I awoke minutes later to find he had already embarked on his journey to New Orleans.

Immediately, a rush of liberation swept through me, and I ran around the house, exclaiming, "Free at last, free at last, he has broken the marriage covenant through desertion; I am free at last." Though unexpected, this newfound freedom filled me with a renewed hope for the future. Even though I was ecstatic that he had left, his sudden and abrupt departure took me back — devoid of any parting courtesies like an embrace, a kiss, or even a simple goodbye, left a deep impression on me.

Compounding my confusion was his complete lack of communication post-departure as he made his way to New Orleans. Not a single call, no text message – this utter absence of contact felt like an additional layer of anguish, exacerbating the burning confusion in my heart. In the wake of such a significant part of our lives, his silence seemed to amplify my request for understanding. It was as if I was dead to him.

I reached out to him the third day after his departure to see if he made it safely to New Orleans and sought understanding and closure; his terse reply of "I can't talk" sent a chill through me.

My further attempts to connect were met with detachment, his distant voice offering no comfort.

As I sat alone in the quiet of our now singular home, I couldn't help but marvel at the change. There was no emotional distance, no stonewalling—only a serene acceptance and a budding hope for my future. CW's departure felt good to me.

It was a sensation I hadn't anticipated, a profound relief bordering on euphoria.

In the days of silence that followed CW's departure, my mind often wandered into a maze of intrusive thoughts. I analyzed the possible reasons behind his abrupt exit and subsequent silence.

Had he met someone in New Orleans when we were there the previous year and departed to be with her? Or were there more profound, complex psychological and emotional factors at play?

Each thought brought a deep emotional weight, casting shadows of doubt about my interaction with him because of how he departed. Something strange happened two weeks after CW left. My initial excitement that he had departed was quickly replaced with an eerie silence in the house and an intense longing for him.

This heavy turmoil in my heart was unlike anything I had ever experienced. It was a mix of relief, grief, and confusion, all swirling in a storm of emotions.

I was perplexed by this intense internal turmoil, a storm within my soul that I couldn't shake off. As I delved into a period of introspection and prayer, earnestly asking the Lord if there was any sin in my life that I needed to confront or repent of, a revelation was gently laid upon my heart.

Through the quiet guidance of the Spirit, He unveiled to me that the agony tearing through me was the result of a soul bond — woven over 33 years of our marriage being irrevocably shattered.

This revelation was not a condemnation but a call to healing. It was a recognition that the pursuit of love for a deep emotional and spiritual connection had been shattered and a reminder of the healing power of God's love.

Realizing the agony stemmed from a shattered 33-year soul bond, I found liberation amidst turmoil, freeing me from toxic chains and guided by the Spirit towards God's grace for solace and direction. I navigated my healing by leaning on the scriptures' profound assurances, particularly the anointing of Jesus to liberate captives and mend bruised hearts as vividly promised in John 4:18, which became a beacon of hope in my darkest moments.

I clung to the belief that in Jesus's completeness, I would find all that was necessary for my contentment. This truth was powerfully affirmed in Colossians 2:10b, which reassured me of my completeness in Christ.

This understanding was further enriched by Jesus's promise in John 6:25, assuring me that my deepest thirsts and cravings would be quenched through Him. These scriptures became my anchor, reminding me of God's faithfulness and promise to His children. By standing firm in God's strength and constantly reminding my Father God of His Word, I anchored my faith in the truth that He is not a man to lie; His promises are yes and amen to those who believe.

As I internalized these promises, which were more than a mere recollection of scripture, it was an intimate engagement with God's Word, allowing its truths to permeate my being as a transformation began to unfold within me as He healed my bruised spirit back to wholeness.

This wholeness ushered in a peace and joy that transcended my circumstances, offering liberation from the chains of despair and loneliness that had once tried to trap me.

This healing power of faith, I realized, was not exclusive to me. It was a gift available to all who sought it, a source of comfort and peace amid life's storms. I am grateful for God's throne in a time of grace to seek His help. It was there, in the sanctity of His presence, that I worshiped Him, pouring out my heart in adoration.

Amid my worship, my focus shifted. I began to pray fervently for CW, proclaiming God's grace and protection over his new life.

I asked God to shine His face upon him, to keep him safe, and to guide him on his path. This act of intercession was not just for CW's benefit but also mine.

It was a way for me to release my hurt and disappointment, let go of the past, embrace the future, and find solace in knowing God was in control of my life.

This meditation was a testament to the transformative power of God's love, compelling me to bless rather than curse, love rather than hate, pray rather than despise, and release rather than hold onto bitterness.

The anointing of Christ broke the shackles binding my spirit, allowing the bruises on my heart to heal and affirming the completeness found in Him. In embracing this truth, I embarked on a journey of abundant grace, rediscovering joy and freedom in the sufficiency of His love. Adopting this method is crucial in your journey toward inner tranquility and healing, particularly after enduring physical abandonment or the dissolution of a marriage.

CW's Journey to Freedom

I was genuinely impressed that CW had finally taken the step. For decades, his actions had hinted at a desire for freedom. His demeanor, often distant and detached, spoke volumes.

Everything about him, from his reluctance to engage with me to his frequent mood changes, seemed to scream of a longing to escape what he perceived as the bondage of our union.

Following CW's departure, amid a whirlwind of emotions, I discovered a sense of pride for CW. I admired CW's courage to pursue a life that aligned with his true self, a decision that led him to leave our marriage, which had ceased to be fulfilling for him.

He finally took to heart my habitual words: if he lacked the desire to work on our marriage if he no longer wanted me, and if the commitment was no longer present, then it was crucial to set me free, or better yet, to set himself free.

CW's decision was not about abandoning our marriage to himself but moving toward his authenticity and happiness. It was a brave step for him, albeit painful, step for me; I don't know if it was painful for him, but it was needed.

I sought explanations on the second occasion we crossed paths after his departure. I asked him why he left without a goodbye and chose silence over communication.

His response was simple: I was asleep, and he didn't want to disturb me. He skirted around the issue of his continued silence—no calls, no texts—and I chose not to push further.

I also asked if someone had influenced his decision to move to New Orleans or if other factors were at play. He explained that relocating to New Orleans had been on his bucket list. Additionally, he mentioned that his move could prove advantageous for my business, which specializes in Twistee Magnetic Hair Ties.

I asked why his departure was secretive, and I was the last to know about his apartment approval. He said he had anticipated my reaction and wanted to avoid confrontation. His explanations left me speechless, though not shocked.

CW often made assumptions, holding onto an image of me that no longer existed—always with an attitude and a sharp retort. I repeatedly pointed out to him that the person he tells himself and others I am is not the truth, and he knows it. Anyone who has ever been around us knows how much I adored that man.

Yet, our perceptions of reality diverge. Where CW sees potential conflict, I see opportunities for communication and understanding.

His departure, while a step towards his liberation, was a blessing in disguise. I know God, as El Elyon, the Most High, exercises sovereignty over everything. I know firmly that nothing in my life happens without God's consent.

I am convinced that God works for the good of those who love Him and are called according to His purpose.

I am profoundly grateful to God for the grace to stay and the faith to finish my journey in my unequally yoked marriage. I was dedicated to upholding my marriage vow to God and CW until death parted us or he freed me from our marital covenant, regardless of CW's reciprocation of love or my unmet needs.

I am deeply thankful for my husband's role in my spiritual journey, pivotal to my transformation. I acknowledge that despite his unbelief, he is an incredible person. I am so proud of him for doing what was suitable for him—however, the secrecy of how he departed was wrong.

Reflecting on this journey, I now see it not merely as a narrative of abandonment and sorrow but as one of resilience and recovery. The lessons on my spirit and soul act as continual reminders of the aftermath following my decision to marry an unbeliever due to my ignorance.

However, these lessons have functioned as the tuition for my path of discipleship, guiding me to live by faith, become a warrior in prayer, use the Word of God as my direction, love God with all my being, sacrifice my desires for Christ, and embrace myself with the divine love that God extends to me.

Embracing a Peaceful New Life

Since my husband's departure, God's care has been evident in unimaginable ways, allowing me to live a fulfilling single life enriched by His presence. I have no regrets; I Just learned lessons. My once fractured heart now brims with gratitude and peace, a testament to the transformative power of faith and God's unwavering love.

To readers, let my marriage be a source of encouragement and insight. If you've given your best doing it Jesus's way and it wasn't enough, you've done all that Jesus requires. Do not blame yourself for outcomes beyond your control. Understand that life has turns we don't expect, but the conclusion is to fear God and keep His commandments.

Remember, despite our best efforts, we cannot control others' decisions, including accepting or rejecting you or Jesus. God loves you deeply and has plans for a more prosperous, profound relationship with Him. May this message uplift you and strengthen your faith in your journey. Life is like a book. Some chapters are sad, and some are happy, but all are necessary for the story.

May you embody the resilience of Abigail, the transformative faith of Rehab, the unwavering patience of Job, the passionate heart of David, the profound wisdom of Solomon, and the boundless love of Christ Jesus as you navigate life, whether with your unbeliever spouse or without them.

CHAPTER 22

Divine Pathway to Healing

Navigating life's hurdles is not a solo journey; it's a partnership with God's grace, a divine force that guides us toward healing. The path to healing in Christ Jesus is a profound transformation that involves acknowledging your pain and being truthful about your emotions. This transformative journey, filled with hope, necessitates patience, faith, and a readiness to entrust your pain to God.

Find solace in the words, 'cast all your anxiety on him because he cares for you' (1 Peter 5:7).

I deeply understand the intricate relationship between spiritual wholeness, mental well-being, and physical health as interconnected avenues to holistic healing. Engaging in self-care practices that nurture my spirit, mind, and body has proven to be a powerful tool for spiritual wellness.

It's not just about prayer and meditation but also about maintaining a healthy lifestyle, cultivating positive relationships, and eliminating stress. This holistic approach underscores the delicate balance between physical health, emotional resilience, and spiritual depth.

Spiritual Wellness

Spiritual wellness is not a static state but a transformative journey that begins with the rebirth of your spirit through faith in Jesus' redemptive death.

It's a path guided by God's grace and the Holy Spirit, where you allow Christ's life to flow through you as you learn from Him. This journey requires prayer, studying God's Word, and applying His teachings. It involves prioritizing God above yourself, worshiping, serving, fasting, and stewardship.

As you grow in the knowledge and grace of Jesus Christ, our Lord, you deepen your understanding and embrace life's challenges with grace and peace, experiencing a profound transformation in your spiritual wellness.

Walking in God's grace and peace signifies a well-nourished spirit. The Apostle Paul, understanding the profound importance of these divine blessings, consistently begins his letters with an invocation of grace and peace from God the Father and our Lord Jesus Christ.

This salutation reflects God's desire for us to experience His grace and peace as fundamental aspects of our lives. Walking in these divine gifts indicates that our lives are in harmony with the Creator's will. This harmony manifests as a well-nourished spirit, a heart at peace, and a mind enriched with divine grace, culminating in a life reflecting God's loving intentions.

Remember, the power to shape your spiritual wellness is in your hands.

Mental Wellness

The path to mental wellness commences with the renewal of the mind through the Word of God after salvation.

As Romans 12:2 states, do not be conformed to this world, but be transformed by the renewing of your mind, that you may prove what *is* that good and acceptable and perfect will of God.

This verse clearly directs the believer: The renewal of your mind is in your hands. Achieving mental wellness starts with a longing for the pure teachings of the Word, much like a newborn craves milk.

It also requires rejecting worldly desires and self-centeredness, urging a transformation in perspective to see things as God does rather than through worldly eyes. For me, this meant turning to God's Word for counsel, effectively making Him my therapist. In this sacred exchange, He provided deep insights into my emotional hurdles, offering healing and clarity.

Actively renewing my mind with His Word, taking Christ's yoke, learning from Him, and obeying His commands have empowered me to develop a deeper understanding and a more resilient approach to overcoming mental oppression and life's challenges while embracing a comprehensive path to mind healing.

It's crucial to understand that while I played a significant part in this journey, the true transformation resulted from the Holy Spirit's power.

The Holy Spirit illuminated the truth from God's Word, convicted me of sin, and empowered me to discern God's good, pleasing, and perfect will. This divine intervention was the catalyst for my mental wellness.

It's crucial to recognize that each individual's journey to mental wellness is unique, as God interacts with us in distinct ways. At the same time, my journey involved God as my therapist and counselor. I relied on His wisdom and strength to navigate mental wellness and life's struggles. By His grace, I could live out the counsel He provided.

However, it's important to acknowledge that others may find essential support in professional therapy or counseling. This professional guidance and spiritual exploration can offer profound insights, aligning psychological healing with spiritual growth. Whether through personal spiritual practices or in conjunction with professional support, embracing the anointing of Jesus is not just a path but the key to mental wellness.

This divine anointing will profoundly transform your mental and emotional well-being when fully embraced.

Physical Wellness:

1 Timothy 4:8 states that physical training is valuable, but godliness has value for all things, holding promise for both the present and future life. This verse guides us towards a balanced approach to physical wellness, recognizing that while caring for our body is crucial, it pales in comparison to the more incredible promise of both current and eternal life. Maintaining physical health through exercise, proper

nutrition, and rest is a personal choice and a responsibility. Being physically healthy contributes to our ability to live fully and serve effectively.

Unfortunately, many prioritize physical health over spiritual and mental wellness, missing the deeper insight that proper health begins with a spiritual one. This is followed by the renewal of the mind for mental stability and, finally, maintaining the physical body—which, despite its importance, is ultimately temporal. This sequence underscores the lasting impact of spiritual health in a holistic approach, reminding us that our bodies, though cared for, will inevitably perish.

In closing, this chapter serves as a testament to the interwoven tapestry of spiritual, mental, and physical wellness. Each facet is crucial, existing independently and complementing one another, forming a holistic approach to health that aligns with God's divine plan.

I hope and pray that you will embrace this divine pathway to healing, allowing God's grace, peace, and wisdom to transform and renew every part of your existence.

CHAPTER 23

Conquering the Consequences

In this final chapter, I reflect on the transformative power of a few challenges from my unequally yoked marriage. I explore the trials I've faced, the lessons I've learned, and how I conquered the consequences. From navigating conflicting values to emotional hurdles, each consequence has allowed growth, resilience, and transformation to cultivate Christ-like characteristics within me.

It has taught me the invaluable virtues of grace, patience, purpose, and unwavering love so I can be God's witness. The tale of a fisherman in the Philippines mirrors my journey. He stumbled upon a colossal pearl, mistaking it for a mere rock, and kept it under his bed for a decade as a lucky charm. When he finally recognized its true worth, he discovered it was valued at one hundred million dollars.

Similarly, I unearthed Christ's purpose within my marriage — a hidden treasure that can be arduous to discern in an unequally yoked relationship. Amidst numerous failures, the divergences in faith and values led to profound struggles. Still, they were God's tools for finding purpose in my marriage and fostering a deeper connection with Him.

The Consequence: The Two Can Never Be One:

The most significant consequence is that my husband and I cannot become one until he surrenders to Christ Jesus. God intended marriage as a means for both partners to grow together spiritually. However, our emotional connection and unity cannot occur without God's Spirit in my spouse. The painful consequence of this disconnect has left a lasting mark on my heart, as we miss out on the profound love that results from learning about each other in the way God intended.

How I Conquered:

I embraced faith as the foundation of my spiritual life, living my faith in the present and hope in the future. In my most profound moments of solitude, prayer was my refuge and strength, anchoring me in my faith. Understanding John 3:16 provided insight into God's love for me, empowering me to live selfless and sacrificial love for Him.

This revelation prompted me to die to myself and live fully in Christ's authority. My journey was marked by a commitment to live a holy life, constantly mindful not to take God's grace in vain. I strove to embody Christ's teachings authentically, finding my spiritual sustenance in Christ, like water in a desert.

Learned Lessons:

- **Prayer as Foundation:** Start with a prayer to tap into spiritual life.

- **Live in Faith and Hope:** Engage with the present and future through faith and hope.
- **God as the Ultimate Fulfiller:** Recognize that only God can satisfy the soul's deepest yearnings.
- **Understanding Unconditional Love:** Learn from John 3:16 about selfless and sacrificial love.
- **Self-Sacrifice for Christ:** To live fully, one must be willing to die for oneself for Christ's sake.
- **Divine Self-Love:** See yourself as God sees you to begin loving yourself divinely.
- **Fulfillment in Christ:** Find your spiritual sustenance in Christ, akin to discovering water in a desert.

The Consequence: Submission in the Face of Contrary Wisdom

Submitting to an unbelieving spouse's decisions presents challenges even when they conflict with one's wisdom. I once faced a situation where my husband's choice involved taking out a loan against our home when we were already facing financial hardship. Despite my reservations, I chose to submit to his decision in line with 1 Peter chapter 3's teachings on submission to unbelieving spouses.

While the outcome was unfavorable, it was a test of my faith. Surrendering my will and trusting in God's bigger plan proved essential. A crucial distinction exists between yielding to my husband's wisdom and yielding to his requests that contradict God's commands.

My allegiance to God's directives precedes compliance with my husband's wishes if they contradict God's command.

How I Conquered:

I learned to value obedience over mere sacrifice, realizing that true submission to God simplifies the most challenging choices. Embracing a meek and gentle spirit, I prioritized the fear of God above my circumstances, finding strength in faithfulness through difficult decisions.

I honed my discernment, which is crucial in distinguishing between genuine submission and mere complicity. Recognizing that it takes two to argue, I chose peace instead, and I disciplined my disappointments, turning them into opportunities for growth and reliance on God. I drew strength from God's presence and sought divine wisdom through consistent prayer and engagement with Scripture, grounding my decisions in God's word rather than the conflicting voices around me.

Learned Lessons:

- **Meek and Gentle Spirit:** Embrace humility and gentleness in all interactions.
- **Value Obedience Over Sacrifice**: True submission to God simplifies choices.
- **Prioritize Fear of God:** Let reverence for God guide you above all circumstances.
- **Strength in Faithfulness:** Remember your convictions, especially during challenges.
- **Power of Prayer:** Use prayer as a primary tool for seeking wisdom and peace.

- **Unexpected Divine Provisions:** Open to God's provision and protection unexpectedly.
- **Discernment Between Submission and Complicity:** Use wisdom to know when to yield and when to stand firm.
- **Avoiding Conflict:** Understand that avoiding unnecessary arguments can lead to peace.
- **Discipline Disappointments:** Transform disappointments into opportunities for spiritual growth.

The Consequence: Foundation on Shaky Ground

In the context of unequally yoked marriages, a fundamental consequence is the inherent instability of its foundation. This instability is vividly illustrated in the words of Jesus from Matthew 7:24-27, where He draws a parallel between building a house on solid rock and constructing one on shifting sand.

In such unions, the home's foundation blends two contrasting elements: the solid rock of Christ Jesus' precepts and the shifting sands of worldly doctrines.

Interestingly, a saved spouse's foundation, firmly rooted in Christ, brings a unique grace to the marriage. (1 Corinthians 7:14)

How I Conquered:

By anchoring myself in God's promises, I found stability in Christ, who became the cornerstone of my marriage. I embraced wisdom and understanding as guiding forces in my life, resisting the urge to let overwhelming circumstances dictate my emotions. I recognized God's grace as it shone brightly in my weakness.

Making deliberate choices, I aligned my life's direction with God's plan, committing to open and honest communication, which is vital for maintaining healthy relationships. I saw my pain as a tool used by God to mold my character to be more like Jesus.

When faced with decisions, I trusted God's 'Noes,' understanding they protected me from my less wise 'Yeses.' I learned the futility of worry, adopting "This, too, shall pass" as a mantra during tough times, which brought comfort and perspective. I learned to appreciate my spiritual portion, find contentment in God's provision, and manage my responses in conversations wisely, choosing peace over conflict.

My pursuit of God's kingdom and righteousness became the key to unlocking all my needs, providing both spiritual and mental fulfillment.

Learned Lessons:

- **Embrace Wisdom and Understanding:** Treat these virtues as close companions in your journey.
- **Resist Circumstances Overwhelming You:** Learn not to let external situations control your inner peace.
- **God's Grace in Weakness:** Lean on God's grace for strength during difficult times.
- **Choice of Spiritual Life:** Actively live by the Spirit rather than the flesh.

- **Importance of Open Communication:** Cultivate honesty and clarity in all your interactions.
- **Purpose in Pain:** Recognize that suffering is not without reason; it shapes and refines us.
- **Protection in Divine Denials:** Trust that when God says no, it's for your protection against misguided choices.
- **Futility of Worry:** Understand the uselessness of anxiety; trust in God's timing.
- **Transience of Troubles:** Remember, "This, too, shall pass."
- **Understanding Your Spiritual Portion:** Know and accept what God has allotted to you.
- **Impact of Present Decisions:** Every choice today shapes your tomorrow.
- **Managing Responses in Conversations:** Choose whether to escalate or soothe tensions in interactions.
- **Seeking Divine Priorities:** Focus on God's kingdom and righteousness to meet all your needs.

The Consequence: A Marriage Lacking Unity

Amos 3:3 poignantly asks, "Can two people walk together unless they agree?" The answer is evident: discordant beliefs can lead to divergent interpretations of God's will and purpose. Disunity creates struggles and prevents peace. The disparity in spiritual natures prevents a true partnership, as fundamental differences in core beliefs and values lead to persistent disagreements, breeding resentment and frustration.

Unequally yoked couples often find themselves at odds; the believing spouse sees the Bible as the ultimate guide for living, whereas the unbelieving spouse explores and values alternate life philosophies. Fundamental disagreements, such as the infallibility of the Bible, further exacerbate the disunity.

How I Conquered:

I sought to emulate Christ's humility and grew in the grace and knowledge of Christ Jesus. By dying to myself and loving God more than myself, I learned to forgive quickly. I recognized that even naive decisions, under God's guidance, could be transformed into valuable lessons.

I harnessed the power of silence to manage my raging emotions and embraced forgiveness to remove spiritual obstacles, allowing love to flow more freely. Viewing trials as opportunities to apply God's forgiveness after failing them, I consulted the Book of Proverbs to sharpen my discernment and avoid deceit.

I minimized complaints to enhance my marriage and responded thoughtfully rather than impulsively, uncovering hidden opportunities in challenges. I tackled bitterness, resentment, and anger by taking back control of my narrative from Satan's influence, choosing instead to feed on Christ's teachings.

Through empathy, I gained clarity and kindness in viewing my partner's perspective. I realized that while love is limitless, it thrives within boundaries that protect its purest forms, and I learned that self-centered love distorts the genuineness of divine love, pushing me toward more selfless love.

Learned Lessons:

- **Transformation of Mistakes:** God can turn ignorant decisions into profound lessons.
- **Power of Silence:** Silence is crucial when emotions are high.
- **Forgiveness as a Pathway:** Clears spiritual blockages, enhancing love's flow.
- **Purpose of Tribulations:** To manifest, mend, and conform us to divine purposes.
- **Importance of Discernment:** Not all that glitters is gold; people can deceive.
- **Impact of Complaining on Relationships:** Complaining strains a marriage.
- **Thoughtful Responses Over Reactions:** Choose to respond thoughtfully to maintain control.
- **Opportunities in Challenges:** Challenges often reveal hidden opportunities.
- **Consequences of Bitterness:** Bitterness and resentment indicate spiritual misalignment.
- **Empathy as Clarity:** Empathy helps see others' perspectives more clearly and kindly.
- **Boundaries in Love:** True love operates within protective boundaries.
- **Selfish vs. Divine Love:** Selfish love hinders the expression of divine love.

The Consequence: Judgment for Upholding Holiness

Living a holy life before God is crucial to our faith, even in an unequally yoked marriage. Striving for peace while upholding our Christian values can be challenging, mainly when our unbelieving spouse's actions and words cause misunderstanding and frustration. This situation can often lead to accusations and misconceptions, such as being perceived as self-righteous or holier than thou.

How I Conquered:

I Embraced the guidance and strength of the Holy Spirit in my daily life. The Holy Spirit empowers me to overcome weaknesses and grow my faith and love for God. I committed to witnessing through my actions, letting my life visibly reflect my faith.

Sanctification through the Spirit came through my struggles as I upheld spiritual disciplines to build my resilience. The Bible was my guide for navigating life's challenges. Its teachings provide direction, comfort, and wisdom. Worship became a vital spiritual booster, reinforcing my connection to God and elevating my spirit.

I practiced giving grace in response to differences, emphasizing living out Jesus' teachings while allowing others to express themselves in their ways. Prioritizing God's approval, I lived with an eternal perspective, enriching my earthly existence. I nurtured my relationship with God daily, strengthening my faith and love for Him.

Recognizing my worth as seen by God, I lived with dignity and purpose, steadfastly committed to a holy life, and confident in the promise of heavenly rewards.

Learned Lessons:

- **Witness Through Actions:** Let your faith be evident in your behavior.
- **Sanctification Through Struggle:** Embrace challenges as opportunities for spiritual growth.
- **Maintaining Spiritual Disciplines:** Consistently uphold practices that deepen your faith.
- **Spiritual Booster: Worship:** Use worship as a source of strength and connection.
- **Grace in Response to Differences:** Extend grace to others, acknowledging diverse perspectives.
- **Emulate Jesus:** Live out Jesus' teachings; let others follow their paths.
- **Value Divine Approval:** Seek God's approval, prioritizing an eternal perspective.
- **The Word of God as My Road Map:** Use the Bible as your guide for navigating life's challenges.
- **Living in the Power of the Holy Spirit:** The Holy Spirit empowers you to overcome weaknesses and live out your faith boldly.
- **Live for the Next Life:** Focus on eternal rewards to gain fulfillment in this life.
- **Daily Relationship Nurturing:** Continuously cultivate your relationship with God.

- **Know and Act on Your Worth:** Recognize your value in God's eyes and act accordingly.
- **Importance of a Holy Life:** Understand that not living a holy life can mean taking God's grace in vain.

The Consequence: Baggage of Mistrust:

CW's previous marriage left him with deep-seated mistrust, creating a pervasive suspicion in our marriage. Despite my continuous efforts to gain his trust, he remained skeptical, often doubting the intentions behind my kindness and love.

How I Conquered:

I learned to let insults slide off like dry mud, recognizing and resisting spiritual oppression by donning the whole armor of God. I deepened my spiritual practices through prayer, fasting, and asserting Christ's authority, placing unwavering trust in God's sovereignty over every situation. I released the past, acknowledging it had already let go of me, and learned to confront issues directly while setting clear boundaries. Regular attendance at church and Bible study fortified me, providing encouragement and guidance. I embraced the truth that you can lead a horse to water but can't make it drink, freeing myself from the bondage of others' strongholds.

In times of confusion and doubt, I stood firm, drawing strength directly from God. I honored my spouse irrespective of my feelings and faced my insecurities empowered by Christ's anointing, cultivating confidence, strength, and resilience. I let God fight my battles, ceased efforts to gain affection from those indifferent, and learned to adjust my crown and persist with dignity.

Learned Lessons:

- **Let Insults Roll Off:** Learn to avoid insults like dry mud.
- **Recognize Spiritual Oppression:** Identify and combat spiritual challenges.
- **Don the Armor of God:** Equip yourself with spiritual protection.
- **Significance of Spiritual Practices:** Emphasize prayer, fasting, and authority in Christ.
- **Trust in Divine Sovereignty:** Have faith in God's ultimate control over situations.
- **Let Go of the Past:** Release past burdens as they have released you.
- **Confront Issues and Set Boundaries:** Address problems directly and maintain clear personal boundaries.
- **Importance of Church Community:** Gain strength and guidance from church and Bible study.
- **Freedom from Bondage:** Do not be enslaved by others' issues.
- **Strength in Confusion:** Rely on God's strength during uncertain times.
- **Honor Commitments:** Maintain respect and honor for relationships regardless of feelings.
- **Overcome Insecurities:** Let Christ's anointing heal your insecurities.

- **Cultivate Patience and Compassion:** Develop qualities that foster understanding and patience.
- **Divine Assistance in Battles:** Let God handle the struggles beyond your control.
- **Release Unreciprocated Care:** Stop pursuing affection from those who are indifferent but continue to love.
- **Adjust Your Crown:** Continue forward with resilience and dignity.

The Consequence: Diverging Financial Paths

Unequally yoked marriages can indeed face significant challenges when it comes to financial views and money management, leading to persistent friction. The disparity between my belief in tithing and viewing our finances collectively versus my spouse's perspective of individual ownership and skepticism towards tithing led to tension. Adopting separate bank accounts emerged as a pragmatic solution to this issue.

How I Conquered:

I committed to not compromising God's principles while remaining flexible on personal preferences and non-essential matters to maintain peace. I valued mutual respect for financial differences and embraced the idea that even a tiny bit of faith can blossom into something vast, akin to a mustard seed growing into a large tree.

I learned to communicate openly about finances without judgment or conflict. Emulating the ant, I practiced diligence, persistence, and preparedness, recognizing that small actions lead to significant achievements. I cultivated gratitude and trust in God's provision, believing that giving is better than receiving. I focused on following Jesus' teachings while allowing others to pursue their own paths.

Learned Lessons:

- **Never Compromise on Core Principles:** Uphold God's principles but remain flexible in personal preferences for peace.
- **Value Mutual Respect in Finances:** Respect differing financial views and practices.
- **Faith Like a Mustard Seed:** Believe that small amounts of faith can grow into substantial impacts.
- **Open Communication About Finances:** Discuss financial matters openly without fighting.
- **Be Diligent Like the Ant:** Small, consistent actions can lead to outstanding achievements.
- **Cultivate Gratitude and Trust:** Always be thankful and trust God's provision.
- **The Blessing of Giving:** Embrace the joy and superiority of giving over receiving.
- **Do Jesus and Let Others Do Themselves:** Live according to Jesus' teachings and let others live according to their beliefs.

The Consequence: Communication Barriers:

CW and I frequently encounter communication barriers due to our differing spiritual natures and worldviews, which are shaped by unique cultural upbringings, personal experiences, and individual belief systems. These differences lead to misunderstandings and misinterpretations in our interactions, making conveying and receiving messages effectively challenging.

How I Conquered:

By venting my frustrations humbly, I release pinned-up emotions. I realized that actions often speak louder than words. I learned the importance of stopping my speech when my words were no longer heard and embraced the value of constructive feedback for my soul. I acknowledged that strategies requiring cooperation are futile if only one person engages.

I found that sometimes, silence can convey more than words ever could. I discovered the power in not always needing the last word and learned that being slow to speak, slow to anger, and quick to listen is vital in mending and nurturing relationships. I became more mindful of my tone of voice, started using "I" statements to express myself without assigning blame, and remained aware of the weight of my words, knowing I must account for them before God.

I chose to wear forgiveness constantly, like a necklace that is never removed. I recognized that my 'but' often hindered the full effect of God's Word in my life. I stopped responding to anger with anger or insults with insults, addressed my emotional triggers, and learned the hard way that words can deeply hurt, especially those that have been swallowed.

Learned Lessons:

- **Vent Frustrations Humbly:** Express frustrations in a controlled and humble manner.
- **Actions Speak Louder Than Words:** Show your intentions and feelings through your actions more than your words.
- **Stop When Not Heard:** Cease speaking if your audience isn't listening; it preserves dignity and respect.
- **Value of Constructive Feedback:** Embrace feedback as it benefits personal growth.
- **Futility of One-Sided Strategies:** Cooperation is vital; solo efforts in joint endeavors are ineffective.
- **Power of Silence:** Recognize that silence can sometimes communicate more effectively than words.
- **Constant Forgiveness:** Treat forgiveness as essential, wearing it always to facilitate continuous freedom in you.
- **Avoid 'Buts' in Faith:** Be mindful of excuses that prevent God's words from fully impacting your life.
- **Not Needing the Last Word:** Find strength in humility and the quiet confidence of letting go.
- **Be Slow and Mindful in Communication:** Enhance relationships by being considerate when communicating.
- **Mindfulness of Tone:** How you say things can be as important as what you say.
- **Use of 'I' Statements:** Speak from personal experience to avoid conflict.

- **Accountability for Words:** Remember that your words carry weight and are accountable to God.
- **Avoid Matching Negativity:** Do not respond to anger or insults with the same, to elevate interactions.
- **Address Emotional Triggers:** Identify and manage what emotionally provokes you for better personal interactions.
- **The Harm in Hurtful Words:** Recognize the lasting impact of harsh words, both spoken and swallowed.

The Consequence: Divergent Parenting Styles

Raising children with a solid moral foundation is crucial for their development and future success. However, when spouses have contrasting approaches to parenting, it leads to challenges. My preference for a biblical approach clashed with my husband's tendency towards leniency, causing discord and confusion in our parenting styles. This lack of unity often led to disagreements and undermined our discipline efforts.

How I Conquered:

I embraced parenting as a profound responsibility with enduring impacts, leaning into the power of fasting, praying, and seeking wisdom to navigate this season. I found strength in identifying the positives in every challenging situation and released my frustrations, continually asking God to sustain my faith throughout the parenting journey.

I have always shared my concerns about our children with CW. My deep love for God enabled me to submit when CW put our children's needs before mine, and I discovered the cathartic power of crying for the soul.

I learned to choose my battles wisely, letting go of trivial conflicts and understanding that human anger does not produce God's righteousness. Despite the challenges of collaborating with my unbelieving spouse, I stood firm in the faith, striving for a compromise that respected our views. I practiced what I preached. I quickly confessed my wrongs and apologized for them rather than rationalizing them.

I adapted my parenting approaches to suit each child's unique needs and embraced God's grace to face the failed tests I had to retake with courage, ready to learn and grow from each experience.

Learned Lessons:

- **Parenting as a Serious Responsibility:** Acknowledge the lasting impact of how you raise your children.
- **Power of Fasting and Prayer:** Utilize spiritual disciplines to strengthen and guide you in parenting.
- **Pray for Wisdom:** Regularly seek divine guidance to navigate parenting challenges.
- **Find Good in Challenges:** Look for positive aspects in difficult situations.
- **Release Frustration:** Avoid negative emotions and maintain faith through parenting trials.
- **Submissive Love:** Be mindful of your husband's position as the head of your home.

- **Crying as Relief:** Understand that expressing emotions through tears can be healing.
- **Choose Battles Wisely:** Focus on significant issues and avoid unnecessary conflicts.
- **Human Anger and Divine Righteousness:** Recognize that personal anger does not fulfill God's standards.
- **Collaborate Despite Differences:** Work towards unity in parenting; never disrespect your spouse in front of the children.
- **Compromise Respectfully:** Find a middle ground that honors both parents' perspectives.
- **Live Your Teachings:** Model the behaviors and values you wish to instill in your family.
- **Adapt Parenting Strategies:** Be flexible in approaches, considering each child's individual needs.
- **Embrace God's Grace:** Recognize the support and forgiveness available to you.
- **Courage in Challenges:** Stay brave and prepared to learn from failures.

The Consequence: Rejection

Rejection in an unequally yoked marriage presents a complex challenge that affects both partners. When one spouse does not share the other's faith, feelings of exclusion and misunderstanding can create significant emotional distance.

This disparity often leads to a unique form of personal and spiritual rejection, impacting how each individual relates to the other and their personal beliefs and values. Navigating this rejection requires a deep understanding of grace and knowing your worth.

How I Conquered:

I recognized that the rejection I faced was not against me but against the Christ within me. I matured emotionally, learning to set aside immediate reactions and anger, and began to see myself as God sees me—worthy of divine love.

I embraced my identity as declared by God and refused to internalize negative words. I committed to loving, blessing, doing good, and praying for my husband. I took responsibility for the atmosphere in our home, choosing God's way of peace over chaos. I resisted the devil, learned not to take things personally, and affirmed my worth.

I walked confidently in my authority in Christ Jesus, embraced the profound truth of dying to live, and found completeness in Christ, who quenched my spiritual and emotional thirst and hunger. I chose to die because I wanted to live in Christ truly. I wrote this book. I modeled behaviors for my children that reflect the values I cherish.

Despite the pain, I found healing in Christ's anointing, focused my heart on heavenly rather than earthly things, and responded to rejection with love, as if for Christ. I eagerly await my crown of righteousness, finding purpose in rejection and seeing one person's rejection as another's treasure. I took my pen back and started writing my own story, letting go of burdens, admitting my mistakes, and learning from them, growing stronger in faith and character.

Learned Lessons:

- **Acceptance in Christ:** Understand that acceptance comes through the Christ within.
- **Emotional Maturity:** Learn to control immediate reactions and manage anger.
- **Divine Self-Perception:** See yourself as God sees you to cultivate self-love.
- **Believe in Your Divine Identity:** Trust what God says about who you are.
- **Reject Negative Words:** Do not internalize harmful speech.
- **Cultivate Love and Prayer:** Actively love, bless, and pray for those who hurt you.
- **Choose Peace:** Control your home's atmosphere by choosing peace over chaos.
- **Resist the Devil:** Stand firm against spiritual oppression.
- **Detachment from Personal Offense:** Learn not to take things personally.
- **Recognize Your Worth:** Know and assert your value.
- **Authority in Christ:** Walk confidently in the authority granted by Christ.
- **Die to Live:** Embrace the paradox of dying to yourself to live in Christ truly.
- **Completeness in Christ:** Find satisfaction in your spiritual identity with Christ.
- **Writing as Healing:** Use writing to process and share your experiences.

- **Model Virtuous Behavior:** Lead by example in teaching values to your children.
- **Healing Through Christ:** Find solace and healing in Christ's anointing.
- **Heavenly Focus:** Prioritize spiritual over earthly concerns.
- **Repaying Hurt with Good:** Treat others kindly, even when they hurt you as if serving Christ.
- **Anticipate Divine Reward:** Look forward to the rewards of righteousness.
- **Purpose in Rejection:** Find valuable lessons and opportunities in rejection.
- **Overcoming Manipulation:** Stop letting others control or manipulate you.
- **Letting Go of Burdens:** Release what holds you back and embrace freedom.
- **Admit and Grow from Mistakes:** Own up to errors and use them as opportunities for growth.

The Consequence: Marriage as a Facade

Maintaining appearances can sometimes create a facade in unequally yoked marriages. Despite seeming harmonious on the outside, there is an underlying emotional and spiritual disconnection.

True unity remains out of reach for couples with unequally yoked natures despite any appearance of togetherness.

There is a difference between living a lie and a façade. Here is an illustration. If I share a photo from my vacation, showing smiles and receiving comments about how great it seems, but in reality, CW and I didn't communicate during the trip and affirm the false perception of happiness, I am living a lie.

In contrast, I openly admit to the lack of interaction with CW during the vacation. I'm not maintaining a facade but being truthful about my marriage. This example demonstrates how the choice of response to others' perceptions can either perpetuate a falsehood or align with the reality of your marriage.

How I Conquered:

I committed to being genuine and transparent, shunning falsehoods and facades. I stopped pressuring CW to want me, learning instead to value myself through loving myself as God loves me. I embraced the power of vulnerability within our marriage to enhance mutual understanding and vowed never to live a lie.

Recognizing God as my ultimate counselor and therapist, I followed His divine guidance as the pathway to peace and victory over the challenges in my marriage.

This spiritual guidance became a powerful tool in navigating our complex relationship. I found joy and contentment in my relationship with God, independent of my spouse's spiritual journey, and I released any negative dispositions that could hinder my walk in love.

I used peace as my measuring rod, refrained from sabotaging myself for the sake of love, and built our home on the foundations of wisdom, understanding, and knowledge.

When I felt taken for granted for following Christ's teachings, I reassured myself that I was on the right path. I rejoiced when persecuted for righteousness, confident in the great reward awaiting me in heaven and the peace I experienced on earth.

Learned Lessons:

- **Value Genuine Transparency:** Avoid falsehoods or facades in all relationships.
- **Self-Value Over External Validation:** Stop pressuring others to fulfill your needs and find worth within yourself.
- **Witness Through Love:** Demonstrate internal and external love as a testimony.
- **Embrace Vulnerability:** Use openness and vulnerability to foster deeper understanding within marriage.
- **Reject Living a Lie:** Commit to honesty, even when presenting a facade, is tempting.
- **Divine Guidance:** Let God guide you as your counselor and therapist, following His advice for peace and victory.
- **Joy in Divine Relationship:** Find contentment in your relationship with God, regardless of your spouse's spiritual journey.
- **Release Negativity:** Let go of negative attitudes that impede your ability to love freely.
- **Peace as a Measure:** Use peace to evaluate decisions and actions in your life.
- **Avoid Self-Sabotage:** Do not compromise your well-being to maintain love.

- **Build on Wisdom, Understanding, and Knowledge:** Use these core principles to lay a solid foundation for your household.
- **Affirm Righteous Actions:** Feel reassured when doing the right thing, even if it feels thankless.
- **Rejoice in Persecution:** When faced with difficulties in doing what is right, celebrate, knowing the rewards are earthly and heavenly.

The Consequence: Loneliness

Loneliness, a profound and often deeply felt consequence, can be a significant challenge in an unequally yoked marriage.

The isolation I've experienced stems not from physical solitude but from the emotional disconnect between us. This disconnect leads to a breakdown in meaningful communication, reduced intimacy, and the sensation of living separate lives instead of sharing a united path. This loneliness has spurred my spiritual growth and transformation.

How I Conquered:

I turned to God for comfort and chose joy, striving to apply God's Word daily and guarding my heart. Throughout these challenges, I embraced God's discipline, recognizing it as an essential part of my growth, not as punishment but as loving correction. I learned to cease efforts to make CW reciprocate my love in the way I expected. I was careful not to share marriage issues publicly that would make either of us uncomfortable if overheard.

Loneliness propelled me to deepen my relationship with God, enhancing my faith and helping me love God more than myself. It allowed me to use solitude for spiritual reflection and growth. This shift helped me see my worth in Christ alone, not relying on my spouse for emotional support, and taught me to love myself as God loves me.

I focused on improving communication and listening skills, recognizing the flesh's weakness but the spirit's willingness. Prayer became my tool for maintaining fidelity and concentrating solely on CW.

I embraced the role of Jesus Christ as my counselor and best friend, finding unique support and understanding. Loneliness also drove me to identify and assert my needs and boundaries within the marriage, preventing resentment and enabling my love to flow more freely.

I used periods of loneliness as opportunities to develop my independence, pursuing personal interests and passions that were fulfilling in their own right. The challenges of feeling alone in my marriage strengthened my resilience, enabling me to handle emotional hardships with more extraordinary grace and stability. Despite the emotional challenges, maintaining a hopeful outlook and focusing on the positives in my life and marriage have been crucial for my mental and emotional health, reinforcing the belief that everything I need is in Christ and accepting God's discipline as part of His loving guidance.

Learned Lessons:

- **Divine Comfort:** Let God be your primary source of comfort in times of distress.
- **Prioritize Divine Conversations:** Talk to God before sharing personal issues with others.
- **Choose Joy:** Actively embrace joy by thinking about God's goodness.
- **Apply God's Word:** Regularly incorporate biblical principles into your decisions and lifestyle.
- **Guard Your Heart:** Protect your emotional and spiritual well-being.
- **Walk in Peace:** Pursue peace in your interactions and personal reflections.
- **Letting Go:** Cease efforts to change others' feelings towards you.
- **Discretion in Sharing:** Avoid discussing anything about your spouse that, if he heard, would cause discomfort.
- **Faith and Prayer:** Deepen your faith and maintain a consistent prayer life.
- **Love God Above All:** Prioritize your relationship with God over all others.
- **Self-Love:** Love yourself as God loves you.
- **Death to Self:** Cultivate selflessness in your daily life.
- **Understanding Personal Needs and Boundaries:** Clearly define and communicate your needs and limits.
- **Transform Loneliness:** Use feelings of loneliness as catalysts for personal growth and independence.

- **Resilience Through Adversity:** Develop strength and endurance through life's challenges.
- **Hope and Positivity:** Maintain a hopeful outlook regardless of circumstances.
- **Embrace Change:** Be open to and accepting changes in your life.
- **Continued Shared Activities:** Keep engaging in activities together, even when challenging.
- **Value God's Discipline:** Do not despise the discipline of the Lord, for it shapes and molds you according to His will.

As I reach the end of this journey, I must reflect on the profound lessons and spiritual growth I've encountered along the way. Conquering the consequences of an unequally yoked marriage has not been about changing my spouse but about transforming myself through God's grace.

It has been about finding strength in vulnerability, peace in turmoil, and joy amid trials. Each challenge has taught me the essence of self-sacrifice, fortified my faith, enriched my prayer life, intensified my love for God and helped me discover the importance of self-love and steadfastness in His Word.

I have learned to walk a path of love and forgiveness, holding fast to the truth that my ultimate partnership is with Christ. In this journey, I've seen that the challenges of being unequally yoked are not roadblocks but divine invitations to embody the virtues of Christ Jesus—to wear patience, understanding, and unconditional love—not just for my spouse but for myself.

As I close this chapter, I carry forward the wisdom that my greatest triumphs often come from my deepest adversities and that every step taken in faith is a step towards a more profound, enduring peace.

Let my story be a teacher and learn through my hardship. Consider this:

- A fool doesn't learn from his mistakes.
- A smart person learns from his mistakes.
- A wise person learns from the mistakes of the fool and the smart person.

Be wise. Learn from my experiences to avoid the complexities of an unequally yoked marriage. Above all, seek God's guidance, live in His truth, and let His grace shape you into the person He designed you to reflect: His Son, Christ Jesus.

ENDNOTES

Chapter 4

1. "G2086 - heterozygeō – Strong's Greek Lexicon (KJV)." Blue Letter Bible. Accessed November 7, 2022. https://www.blueletterbible.org/lexicon/g2086/nkjv/tr/0-1/

2. Steve Higginbotham, "Unacceptable Statistics," Preaching Help, February 13, 2011, https://preachinghelp.org/unacceptable-statistics

3. Kay Arthur, Lord, I Want to Know You (Multnomah, 1996)

Chapter 6

1. Spiros Zodhiates, "Justified and Unjustified Anger 1 of 3," November 17, 2012. https://www.youtube.com/watch?v=89r8ZxEw_6k

2. "G3709 - orgē – Strong's Greek Lexicon (KJV)." Blue Letter Bible. Accessed July 20, 2022. https://www.blueletterbible.org/lexicon/g3709/kjv/tr/0-1/

3. "G2372 - thymos – Strong's Greek Lexicon (KJV)." Blue Letter Bible. Accessed July 20, 2022. https://www.blueletterbible.org/lexicon/g2372/kjv/tr/0-1/

4. "G1401 - doulos – Strong's Greek Lexicon (KJV)." Blue Letter Bible. Accessed July 20, 2022. https://www.blueletterbible.org/lexicon/g1401/kjv/tr/0-1/

5. Dr. Spiros Zodhiates, Work of Faith—an Exposition of James 1:1□2:13 (William B. Eerdmans, 1959) 14.

Chapter 7

1. "G4049 - perispaō – Strong's Greek Lexicon (KJV)." Blue Letter Bible. Accessed July 21, 2022. https://www.blueletterbible.org/lexicon/g4049/kjv/tr/0-1/

2. Kendra Cherry, "Loneliness: Causes and Health Consequences," Very Well Mind, May 24, 2022, https://www.verywellmind.com/loneliness-causes-effects-and-treatments-2795749

3. Kay Arthur, James □ A Faith That's Real (Precept Ministries, 1971)

Chapter 8

1. "G4647 - skolops – Strong's Greek Lexicon (kjv)." Blue Letter Bible. Accessed July 21, 2022. https://www.blueletterbible.org/lexicon/g4647/kjv/tr/0-1/

Chapter 10

1. "H8669 - tᵊšûqâ – Strong's Hebrew Lexicon (KJV)." Blue Letter Bible. Accessed September 16, 2022. https://www.blueletterbible.org/lexicon/h8669/kjv/wlc/0-1/

Chapter 13

1. Kay Arthur, Lecture series on 1 Peter (Precept Ministries, 1992)

www.ingramcontent.com/pod-product-compliance
Lightning Source LLC
Chambersburg PA
CBHW050857160426
43194CB00011B/2190